Israel Rosenfield

THE STRANGE,
FAMILIAR, AND FORGOTTEN

Israel Rosenfield, who holds an M.D. from New
York University and a Ph.D. in intellectual history from Princeton University, teaches at the
City University of New York. He is the author
of *Freud: Character and Consciousness*, *The
Invention of Memory: A New View of the Brain*,
and *DNA for Beginners* (with Edward Ziff).

Also by Israel Rosenfield

•

Freud: Character and Consciousness

DNA for Beginners (with Edward Ziff)

The Invention of Memory: A New View of the Brain

THE STRANGE,

FAMILIAR, AND FORGOTTEN

THE STRANGE,
FAMILIAR, AND FORGOTTEN

An Anatomy of Consciousness

ISRAEL ROSENFIELD

Vintage Books
A Division of Random House, Inc.
New York

FIRST VINTAGE BOOKS EDITION, APRIL 1993

Copyright © 1992 by Israel Rosenfield

All rights reserved under International and Pan-American Copyright
Conventions. Published in the United States by Vintage Books, a division of
Random House, Inc., New York, and simultaneously in Canada by
Random House of Canada Limited, Toronto. Originally published in hardcover
by Alfred A. Knopf, Inc., New York, in 1992.

Library of Congress Cataloging-in-Publication Data
Rosenfield, Israel, 1939–
The strange, familiar, and forgotten: an anatomy of consciousness /
Israel Rosenfield.
p.   cm.
Includes bibliographical references and index.
ISBN 0-679-74305-7 (pbk.)
1. Neuropsychiatry—Philosophy.   2. Consciousness.   I. Title.
RC343.R76   1993
153—dc20   92-50651
CIP

Book design by Anthea Lingeman

Manufactured in the United States of America
10 9 8 7 6 5 4 3 2 1

In memory of
Jacob Rosenfield
and
Nadia and Léon Temerson

Ce que j'ai appris, je ne le sais plus. Le peu que je sais encore, je l'ai deviné.

(All that I've learned, I've forgotten. The little that I still know, I've guessed.)

—Chamfort, *Maximes et pensées*, 1795 (posthumous)

Une mode ancienne demeure une curiosité; une mode passée depuis peu devient un ridicule; une mode régnante qu'anime la vie nous semble la grâce même.

(An old fashion remains a curiosity; a fashion but late gone by becomes an absurdity; a reigning fashion, full of life, strikes us as the very personification of grace.)

—Octave Uzanne, *Les Modes de Paris*, 1898

Le cerveau de l'enfant, c'est la terre sur laquelle la charrue ne trace pas vainement son sillon fertilisateur. Le cerveau de l'aphasique, c'est la mer où la proue du navire ne peut pas laisser sa trace.

(The child's brain is land on which the plow does not trace in vain its fertilizing line. The aphasic's brain is a sea where the ship's prow cannot leave its mark.)

—Armand Trousseau

Il n'y a de nouveau que ce qui est oublié.

(Nothing is new, only forgotten.)

—Rose Bertin, dressmaker for Marie-Antoinette

Our thought is fluctuating, uncertain, fleeting, successive, and compounded; and were we to remove these circumstances, we absolutely annihilate its essence.

—David Hume, *Dialogues Concerning Natural Religion*, 1779

Contents

Acknowledgments

It was an immense privilege to work with Elisabeth Sifton, whose intelligence and understanding certainly made this a better book. I am deeply thankful to her, and to Martine Desi, Oliver Sacks, and Catherine Temerson for helping and inspiring me.

THE STRANGE,

FAMILIAR, AND FORGOTTEN

I

<hr>

Consciousness:
The Major Business of the Brain

What we say and do often hides motives that we keep from others and even from ourselves. Modern psychology began when this observation, as old as the writing of history, was turned into a principle: that our thoughts and actions are to a great extent determined by ideas, memories, and drives that are unconscious and inaccessible to conscious thought; that unknowable forces determine our actions. Thus the study of the unconscious became the cornerstone of twentieth-century psychology. Consciousness itself was ignored, since after all elucidating the unconscious seemed to tell us so much. People came to presume that when they talked of their "memories," they meant experiences and learning that were carefully stored away in their brains and could be brought into consciousness, or made conscious. But this was to ignore the possibility that memories were in fact part of the very structure of consciousness: not only can there be no such thing as a memory without there being consciousness, but consciousness and memory are in a certain sense inseparable, and understanding one requires understanding the other.

Indeed, the more we learn about the complex structure of

consciousness, the more we are forced to abandon many received ideas about memory and the nature of thought and action. A reexamination of the neurological evidence gives us powerful reasons, I believe, to address one of the most interesting—and long-neglected—questions we can ask about ourselves: What is the nature and structure of our consciousness? We cannot yet answer the question with any great precision, but then we have also been unable to elucidate where and how memories are stored in our brains, and our failure to do so may not be an accident: human memory may be unlike anything we have thus far imagined or successfully built a model for. And consciousness may be the reason why.

What makes consciousness puzzling and hard to talk about is its utter subjectivity, the uniqueness of each individual human perspective. For example, you may note with pleasure (or irritation) the apparent agreement when I exclaim, "I was just thinking the same thing!" because you know—we all know—how remarkable it seems when someone with very different experiences and attitudes has virtually the same insight as oneself. We are moved by the pain and suffering of other people, not because we have known exactly their experience, but because we know the terrible sense of isolation and helplessness in the individual experience of pain; we know its subjectivity, its unique personal roots. What fascinates us about one another is seeing objectively, in one another, the very responses to experience that we also know to be so subjective and special. If we *really* knew the thoughts and feelings, sufferings and joys, of other people just as they know them, there would be no surprise, no sense of discovery or newness; we would not be moved or interested. But instead we are amazed by the common ground it is possible to establish; similar thoughts and feelings can apparently occur to others, so different from ourselves, in *their* subjectivity. In crowd situations, when a group of people strongly sense that they are sharing a feeling—for example, when we are moved to tears or laughter by a play in unison with all the other members of the audience—we are excited and charmed by the group feeling, but that sense of oneness evaporates very quickly, and we return to our individual selves well before we exit from the theater. Then we may try to convince one another of our own personal responses to the play, even manipulate one another's reactions, but at heart we know this effort is futile, which is one reason it is so fascinating.

We can no more capture the essence of our own subjectivity than we can capture that of others. For to say that consciousness is subjective is also to say that it is dynamic and ever changing; our subjective experience is made up of unreproducible, evolving mutually dependent states of mind, knowable only from our own unique perspectives.

In this subjectivity, oddly, we nonetheless feel or believe we are experiencing the objective truth about the world, and we call that knowledge; we usually think of knowledge as something that can be understood and also transmitted from one person to another. This in turn has given rise to the belief, widely held by scientists and philosophers, that our brains in some sense re-create images of the objects we perceive (though not necessarily in a "pictorial" form). Neurophysiological studies of the brain have shown, for example, that different areas of brain tissue appear to respond to specific kinds of visual information such as colors, shapes, and motion. And while no scientist has yet explained how or why such a neural response becomes conscious awareness, it is nevertheless assumed that the brain is in one way or another doing something with the visual perceptions that somehow leads to consciousness of them.

However, if one thinks about the ordinary human experience of being conscious, of being aware and alert to the meaning of one's ongoing experiences, it seems unlikely that perceptions become conscious by these re-creations or representations in the brain, however complex they are supposed to be. This notion presupposes a static model of brain function; but consciousness has a temporal flow, a continuity over time, that cannot be accounted for by the neuroscientists' claim that specific parts of the brain are responding to the presence of particular stimuli at a given moment. Our perceptions are part of a "stream of consciousness," part of a continuity of experience that the neuroscientific models and descriptions fail to capture; their categories of color, say, or smell, or sound, or motion are discrete entities independent of time. But more importantly, I believe, a sense of consciousness comes precisely from the *flow* of perceptions, from the relations among them (both spatial and temporal), from the dynamic but constant relation to them as governed by one unique personal perspective sustained throughout a conscious life; this *dynamic* sense of consciousness eludes the neuroscientists' analyses. Compared to it, units of "knowledge" such as we can transmit or record in books or images are but instant snapshots taken in a dynamic flow of uncontainable, unrepeatable, and inexpressible experience. And it is an unwarranted mistake to associate these snapshots with material "stored" in the brain.

The comparison with snapshots versus a film with a soundtrack is perhaps more than a mere metaphor. Motion pictures give us a sense of continual movement by means of a series of static images presented in rapid succession, but our conscious visual experience is not of one static image followed by another; instead we see motion because we relate one image to the next; the impression of motion is a consequence of the brain's processing the relation between the one image and the next and the next. To put it more precisely, the consciousness of motion comes from the brain's relating one set of stimuli to the next set. (That we comprehend motion when the static images are presented at the rate of twenty-four frames per second but, at any slower rate, see only a succession of static frames, suggests that the brain establishes consciousness in terms of stimuli occurring about twenty-fourths of a second apart.)

Similarly, consciousness of a static object is relational, too. The static image is perceived over time, after all, just as with a moving object or with shifting images, and the brain is once again processing sets of stimuli over time, relating one to the next and the next, establishing awareness of (in this case) the image's unchanged, unmoving reality. It is this relating, this connecting between moments—not the moments themselves—that is consciousness. Conscious perception is temporal: the continuity of consciousness derives from the correspondence which the brain establishes from moment to moment. Without this activity of connecting, we would merely perceive a sequence of unrelated stimuli from moment to unrelated moment, and we would be unable to transform this experience into knowledge and understanding of the world. This is why conscious human knowledge is so different from the "knowledge" that can be stored in a machine or in a computer.

If awareness, or consciousness, thus emerges from a constantly evolving relation among sets of stimuli, then may we argue that our memories similarly rise to consciousness? That like the perception of motion created from static images, we recollect by means of stored images of one kind or another being related in the brain in this way? But how then do we tell the difference between a recollection and a direct perception? True, hallucinations blur this difference or eliminate it, but one cannot argue that we hallucinate our memories; we all know that the mental experience of an ordinary memory is different from that of a hallucination, let alone that of an immediate perception. No, conscious memory, like all conscious acts, is and has to be relational, and the nature of the relation is different from that in direct perception, although direct perception depends on it. The vital ingredient is self-awareness. My memory emerges from the relation between my body (more specifically, my bodily sensations at a given moment) and my brain's "image" of my body (an unconscious activity in which the brain creates a constantly changing generalized idea of the body by relating the changes in bodily sensations from moment to moment). It is this relation that creates a sense of self; over time, my body's relation to its surroundings becomes ever more complex, and, with it, the nature of myself and of my memories of it deepen and widen, too. When I look at myself in a mirror, my recognition of myself is based on a dynamic and complicated awareness of self, a memory-laden sense of who I am. It is not that my memories exist as stored images in my brain, conscious or unconscious; the act of memory is one of my relating to myself, or to others, or to past experiences, or to previously perceived stimuli. This is the very essence of memory: its self-referential base, its self-consciousness, ever evolving and ever changing, intrinsically dynamic and subjective. Indeed, perception in general, conscious awareness of one's surroundings, is always from a particular point of view, and is only possible when the brain creates a body image, a self, as a frame of reference.

Scientists can, to some extent, document certain changes in this subjectivity. Brain damage limits the subjective worlds of the patients who have suffered the traumas. Traditionally, neurologists and psychologists have argued that in the classic cases, the disease or trauma in the brain destroyed specific memories, or limited certain of the patient's capabilities. This book challenges that view; for it is not possible to lose specific memories without profound alterations in the entire structure of an individual's knowledge. I shall argue, rather, that the clinical studies reveal these profound alterations in the patients' consciousness. If we study the neurological cases in the light of that hypothesis, they suggest a view of knowledge, memory, and understanding that is at odds with much of the conventional wisdom that neurologists, psychologists, and even philosophers have advanced over the past century. And what emerges from this reevaluation is a richer, deeper understanding of human psychology and its origins in the mechanisms of the brain.

One of the earliest discussions about the nature of memory and consciousness dates from the late eighteenth century, when William Molyneux wrote to John Locke wondering if a man born blind would be able to see if he suddenly recovered his sight. At the heart of his query was the issue of the real nature of experience, memory, and consciousness. Suppose, Molyneux wrote, the man had been

> taught by his touch to distinguish between a cube and a sphere of the same metal. Suppose then the cube and the sphere were placed on a table, and the blind man made to see: query, whether by his sight, before he touched them, could he distinguish and tell which was the globe and which the cube? The acute and judicious proposer answers: not. For though he has obtained the experience of how the globe, how the cube, affects his touch, yet he had not yet attained the experience that what affects his touch, so or so, must affect his sight, so or so.[1]

Molyneux's question was first answered with clinical evidence almost four decades later, when an English surgeon, William Cheselden, removed cataracts from the eyes of a thirteen-year-old boy, permitting him to see for the first time in his life. The boy's initial reaction was that his eyes appeared to be "touching" objects presented to him, and he found that the objects were disproportionately large. He had no sense of distance. A small object placed in front of him appeared as large as a house at a great distance; and his bedroom seemed to him to be as large as the house of which it was a part, though he knew that this was not possible. He would look at a cat and a dog and ask which one was the cat and which the dog, until he finally stroked one of the animals, reflecting, "The next time I will know your name." Cheselden wrote:

We thought he soon knew what pictures represented which were shewed to him, but we found afterwards we were mistaken; for about two months after he was couched, he discovered at once they represented solid bodies, when to that time he considered them only partly-coloured planes, or surfaces diversified with variety of paint; but even then he was no less surprised, expecting the pictures would feel like the things they represented, and was amazed when he found those parts, which by their light and shadow appeared now round and uneven, felt only flat like the rest, and asked which was the lying sense, feeling or sight?[2]*

* Richard Gregory and J. G. Wallace describe a more recent study of a similar case in their *Recovery from Early Blindness: A Case Study*. Their patient had great difficulty seeing objects in paintings and was unable to make sense of cartoon drawings of faces. Mirrors fascinated him, perhaps because, before recovering his sight, he was like the blind man Diderot describes, in his *Lettre sur les aveugles*, who could conceive of mirrors only as machines that create three-dimensional images of ourselves: "*un miroir est une machine qui nous met en relief hors de nous-même.*" The patient's sense of self, and of his relation to the world, was profoundly altered by his ability to see himself in a mirror.

Indeed, which was the lying sense? Cheselden's patient knew that cats and dogs exist, and he knew that a room could not be as large as the house of which it was a part. He did not understand how a two-dimensional representation could look like a three-dimensional object. He was confused because he was unable to make sense of his surroundings.

Lack of experience (Cheselden's patient certainly lacked visual experience) or loss of memory can in part explain such confusion or failure to understand. But confusion and understanding are aspects of conscious behavior, indeed they are states of consciousness, suggesting very different sets of relations between the individual and the world, and there is no way to grasp what they are without some idea of what we mean by consciousness. Computers, for example, which lack consciousness, do not become confused when they arrive at contradictory conclusions or when part of their "memory" is lost; it might also be said that they never "understand" what they are doing.

Of course, one could argue that the Cheselden patient's confusion was a psychological consequence of the lack of agreement between his visual and tactile senses. And one could say that were we to work out a way of adding "consciousness" to the computer, it, too, would show confusion or, alternately, feel contentment when everything "fit" and it "understood." Perhaps this is true, but at the moment there is no reason to believe it. On the contrary, cases like Cheselden's suggest the inadequacy of the computer model and hint that there is something profoundly wrong with our conventional mechanical ideas about memory and experience. When Cheselden's patient wondered which was the lying sense, the tactile or the visual, he was noting that independently each sense carried absolute conviction. What was confusing was not the lack of agreement between the senses, but the certainty with which his senses allowed him to reach opposing conclusions. No machine is *troubled* by, or even *intrigued* by, feelings of certainty that appear contradictory. The neurological evidence is in fact telling us as much about consciousness as it is about memory, and it is telling us, further, that they seem to be part of the same grand structure.

Yet mechanical ideas about the mind (which predate the invention of the computer) are very powerfully entrenched, and neurologists and psychologists have long treated patients as if their consciousness were but a minor attribute of mental functioning. As one contemporary psychologist has written:

> Psychology has been understandably wary of returning to consciousness, and has done so only with an array of new techniques. But it is already clear that the role of consciousness in mental life is very small, almost frighteningly so. The aspects of mental life that require consciousness have turned out to be a relatively minor fraction of the business of the brain, and we must consider consciousness to be a brain system like any other, with particular functions and properties. It looms large only in our introspection.[3]

Still, one type of mental activity, and hardly a minor one, that requires consciousness is remembering; without memory we could never know what we have learned. The problem is that we have tended to think of memories as unconscious items that one brings to consciousness, not as *part* of consciousness. But after all, it is conscious behavior that gives us reason to believe that memories exist. So we have to understand consciousness before we can assume that memories simply "rise" to it or are tacked onto it; it must be ascertained whether memory and consciousness are part of the same structure or not.

Nor can we understand the unconscious processes of the brain without understanding consciousness. Our knowledge of the unconscious is derived from observations of conscious behavior, after all. The problem is analogous to the famous discussion in physics as to the nature of light: is it made up of particles or waves? With measuring devices that are sensitive to waves (interference gratings, for example), light manifests itself as waves; with measuring devices sensitive to particles (photoelectric cells), light manifests itself as particles. So is light particle or wave? It is *neither*; it is simply that we see it as one or the other, depending on the measuring apparatus. So, too, our conscious life suggests that we have memories stored in our brains, but when we try to find where or how they are stored we fail to find the traces of them, and some aspects of our mental life (dreams, for example) suggest that conscious and unconscious forms of memory may be quite different. Actually they are both part of a larger structure, and they manifest themselves in very different ways, depending on circumstances. An essential part of that larger structure is consciousness.

The idea of consciousness as merely the minor business of the brain has a long history. For the ancients, consciousness—conscious knowledge, thought, and feeling—was too important to attribute to anything so mundane as the brain, indeed to any body organ. Aristotle, for example, believed that the rational soul, the basis of thought, was immaterial. In the Middle Ages, too, the substance of the brain was ignored; common sense and imagination, pure thought, and memory were attributed to "spirits" residing in the three largest fluid-filled spaces in the brain, known as ventricles. (A fourth, smaller space was generally ignored.) Even so acute an observer as Leonardo da Vinci drew a schematic view of the ventricles that justified such a perception.

In the seventeenth century, René Descartes (1596–1650) claimed that the immaterial soul, responsible for thought and feeling, or consciousness, resided in the pineal gland, where it came in contact with the "vital spirits" and thus controlled the material body. The soul was pure thought. Descartes's famous dictum, "I think therefore I am," means: I exist only so long as I think; if I cease to think I cease to exist; thinking is immaterial and does not need a body to exist. The brain, in Descartes's view, was a machine that governed the body; it worked "every bit as naturally as the movements of a clock or other automaton." Like all machines, it could be studied, but it had nothing to do with thought or consciousness.[4]

Later in the century, the English physician Thomas Willis (1621–1675) suggested that the brain, and in particular the prominent left and right hemispheres (the cerebral hemispheres) which constitute seventy percent of the total brain substance in humans, in some way initiated thought and action. But Willis concluded that these "higher" functions must be separate from the parts of the brain concerned with mundane activities such as walking and other simple motor activities and that there was no anatomical connection between the brain's higher and lower centers. Even as late as the nineteenth century, these connections, which in the actual tissues are not difficult to discern, were overlooked by anatomists blinded by philosophical preconceptions.

A radically new view of the brain was suggested by one of the nineteenth century's great neuroanatomists, Franz Gall (1758–1828), who postulated that implicitly, at least, the creation and maintenance of consciousness was that organ's most important and pervasive function. But in an ironic twist, Gall's theory came to be used to justify the idea, in opposition to his own view, that consciousness is but a minor and "particular" function of the brain.

Gall was more influential in the salons and cafés of nineteenth-century Paris than in the scientific circles of his day. Born in Baden, he studied in Strasbourg and then Vienna, where he subsequently began his teaching career. On December 25, 1801, the Hapsburg emperor, Frederick II, prohibited Gall from teaching and publishing his "doctrine about heads,"[5] organology, lest "some lose their heads over it." Gall later moved to Paris, where he had an enormous success in the *haut monde*.

Gall argued that the brain is a complex mosaic of mental organs. Each organ has a specific mental function and anatomical location. The mental organs are located in the cerebral convolutions, the twisted, tubelike surface of the brain, which anatomists had often compared to the intestines. The larger a convolution in a particular brain, the more important was that mental organ in the individual's personality. This, Gall claimed, explained human individuality, since the relative size and importance of the different organs varied (because of innate, or genetically determined, factors) from individual to individual.

Gall's original text suggested that twenty-seven basic mental faculties had specific anatomical localizations in the brain. (He later expanded this to thirty-one. See list on pages 16–17.) In the light of subsequent developments in neurology, note should be made especially of the following in Gall's list: memory of facts and things; sense of spatial relations; memory for people; sense of words and names, or verbal memory; sense of spoken words, or philological gifts. Consciousness is, at least implicitly, an essential attribute of these and all the other facilities on Gall's list.

So is memory: "Perception and memory are only attributes common to the fundamental psychical qualities, but not faculties in themselves," Gall wrote. Each mental organ has its

Gall's Mental Functions and Their Localizations[6]

Combativeness, Courage, Fighting Instinct, Aggressive Instinct, Tendency to Oppose · posterior part of inferior temporal convolution

Carnivorous Instinct, Destructiveness, Propensity to Annihilate, Impulse of "Anger," Irascibility · middle part of the inferior temporal convolution

Hoarding Instinct, Sense of Property, Acquisitiveness, Propensity to Make Provision · superior anterior part of the temporal lobe, behind Constructiveness

Cautiousness, Foresight, Circumspection, Emotion of Fear, Organ of Melancholy · supra-marginal convolution

Constructiveness · anterior edge of temporal lobe, in front of Acquisitiveness

Propensity of Propagation, Sexual Instinct · Cerebellum

Love of Offspring, Parental Love · lower part of occipital lobe, near the middle line

Attachment, Social Affection · occipital lobe, external to Parental Love

Inhabitiveness, Attachment to Home and Country · occipital lobe, above Parental Love

Pride, Love of Authority, Self-Esteem · superior parietal lobule, near the middle line

Vanity, Love of Approbation, Love of Glory · superior parietal lobule, external to Self-Esteem

Firmness, Perseverance, Obstinacy · top of the posterior central convolution, behind the Fissure of Rolando

Verbal Memory · Island of Reil

Linguistic Faculty · posterior part of orbital convolutions

Memory of Objects, Educability · lower end of first frontal convolution

Memory for Moving Things, Memory of Events · above the former in first frontal convolution

Memory of Persons, Perception of Form · anterior part of orbital convolutions, near middle line

Memory of Spaces and Places, Relation of Objects in Space · lower end of second frontal convolution

Color Sense · orbital convolutions, central and anterior

Faculty of the Relation of Numbers, Memory for Numbers · anterior outer part of the orbital convolutions

Tone Sense, Music · within the Fissure of Sylvius at anterior edge of temporal lobe

Time Sense, Music · not located

Comparative Sagacity, Deductive Faculty, Perception of Similitude · middle of the first frontal convolution, above Memory for Facts and Events

Metaphysical Sagacity, Causality, Inductive Faculty, Aptitude for Drawing Conclusions · middle part of second frontal convolution, at side of Comparison

Wit, Humor, Perception of Dissimilitudes · outer margin of second frontal convolution: in center, external to Causality

Poetical Aptitude, Ideality, Creative Fancy · upper part of third frontal convolution

Sense of Fine Arts; the Perfecting, Aesthetic Faculty; Sense of Beauty · not located

Imitation, Tendency to Copy, Mimicry · ascending frontal convolution, below Veneration

Sympathy, Benevolence, Compassion, Good Nature · most posterior part of first frontal convolution

Religious Sense, Veneration · upper part of ascending frontal convolution

Visionary Capacity, Wonder, Inspiration, Prominent in Fanatics · not located

own way of functioning, its own structure of knowledge; knowledge of music is different in kind (and structure) from knowledge of architecture. And therefore the nature of the consciousness, perception, and memory associated with each function is different, he believed; perceiving and remembering music require very different processes from perceiving and remembering architecture: "Thus attention, perception, memory, judgment and imagination are nothing else than the different modes of action of every one of the fundamental capacities." This explains why one person might have a good memory for music and a very poor one for poetry. "One man remembers facts and forgets dates; another recollects faces and not names; some never lose from their minds the places where they have been yet have no power to recall a tune; therefore, memory is not a simple fundamental faculty." In other words, memory is an integral part of each mental faculty, and its very nature differs from faculty to faculty; memory is not a recording of an "image" or a "trace" but part of the *process* of knowing and understanding, which differs in each faculty or mental organ.[7]

The ultimate test of the truth or falsehood of Gall's view of memory was, as we shall see, the study of clinical syndromes. As early as 1825, the French physician Jean-Baptiste Bouillaud (1796–1875) wrote that Gall's views were supported by a number of clinical observations. Lesions localized in an area of the brain called the frontal lobes of the brain, for example, often damaged what Bouillaud called the "legislative organ of speech," resulting in the loss of speech. He suggested that the ability to understand words was determined by tissue that was separate from that needed to articulate words. Though a considerable number of clinical reports supported Bouillaud's claims, most physicians paid little attention to his work; Gall's theory, they believed, had nothing to do with medicine. Some ten years later, Bouillaud's observations were given greater precision; the French physician Marc Dax (1771–1837) reported that speech difficulties were almost always associated with damage to the left side of the brain. Again, Dax's report was of so little interest to the medical world that it remained in the archives of the Montpellier Medical Society until the 1860s, when Dax's son recalled his father's observations to an audience that no longer held Gall's ideas in contempt.

The scientist who was most responsible for the reversal of Gall's reputation was Paul Broca (1824–1880). On April 17, 1861, Broca gave a demonstration of a brain-damaged patient to the Société d'Anthropologie, of which Broca was a founder and leading member, a group known for its left-wing political and anticlerical views. Broca's patient had lost his speech twenty-one years earlier; he was known as "Tan" because this was the one syllable that he could utter. (His real name was Leborgne—which means "one-eyed.") He had no paralysis of the tongue or lips and appeared to be able to understand what was said to him. His speech loss, Broca noted, was caused by damage to a well-circumscribed area in the left hemisphere of the brain, known today as Broca's area. Broca had discovered the speech center of the brain, or, as Gall would have said, the speech organ. More than thirty years after his death, Gall had been vindicated.

Then, in 1874, Gall's work was undermined, and consciousness disappeared from the concerns of the medical world. In that year Carl Wernicke published *The Symptom Complex of Aphasia: A Psychological Study on an Anatomical Basis.* Wernicke noted that patients with damage to Broca's area either were unable to speak, as in the case of Tan, or could, at best, produce sentences that lacked grammatical structure. Most characteristic was their failure to use connective words such as "if," "and," and "but"; they found it extremely difficult to repeat the phrase "No ifs, ands, or buts." Rather than say something like "I will come to New York," they would say "I New York come." Yet they appeared to have little or no difficulty understanding what was said to them.

Another group of patients, Wernicke noted, had fluent, grammatical speech, but it seemed to lack specific content, such as the sentence "Before I was here I was there and then they came and I was here." Specific references ("fork") were replaced by roundabout phrases ("the thing you put in the meat"). And these patients understood nothing that was said to them. In the nineteenth century, such patients were often treated as lunatics (even today they are sometimes misdiagnosed as psychotic). In fact, they were suffering from damage to a specific area of the brain, known today as Wernicke's area.

One would have thought that Wernicke had discovered another example of what Gall called the organs of the brain. Not at all, Wernicke argued. Gall had been mistaken to assume that complex mental functions could be anatomically localized. All that could be localized were the "memories" of words—he called localized "memories" elementary psychic processes—in the form either of "auditory word images" (essential for understanding spoken words) or of "motor word images" (essential for speaking). Broca's patient Tan, for example, had lost his motor word images (stored in Broca's area); he was unable to articulate the sounds of words, though his auditory word images were intact and his understanding of speech was unaffected. Patients with damage to Wernicke's area, on the other hand, had lost auditory word images; they could not understand speech, though they had no difficulty in speaking, and their speech was empty because they could not understand what was going on around them.

Though Wernicke believed that memories were simply stored "images" that the brain could use at appropriate moments, he left unclear why the brain would choose to store one image rather than another, or how it decided which images were appropriate in given circumstances and should be brought to consciousness. Nor did he explain how an image became conscious. Was the conscious image the same as the unconscious one? Was a memory like an electric sign sitting inside the brain waiting to be turned on? Scientists and psychologists even today speak of unconscious memories becoming conscious as if it were little different from flipping on a lamp switch. And while they often say that conscious memories may be "distorted" or incomplete forms of their unconscious counterparts, they fail to recognize that the notion of a distorted memory makes sense only if one has a coherent account of the nature of consciousness.

Another important factor often overlooked is that the failure of memory in a patient with brain damage is quite different from everyday failures of memory, from our ordinary experience of forgetting. When I say to a person, "I'm sorry, but I don't remember your name," I am saying: "I *know* you have a name and I once knew the name, but I cannot bring it forth at the moment." Though it is temporarily irretrievable, it is still, in some sense, a part of my knowledge in general. After all, when you tell me your name, I will instantly recognize it. And if I never knew your name, I will learn it and remember it (and perhaps later forget it). Memory losses owing to brain damage are quite different. Some patients do not know that they once knew a particular name or fact; for them, the memory does not and never did exist—they experience it not as something that has been forgotten but as something that was never known *and that is not knowable*; it does not and cannot make any sense; it cannot exist. The patient cannot learn the name or the fact; it does not fit into the structure of his or her knowledge of the world. Patients with a specific injury may, for example, treat everything on the left side of their body as nonexistent, though they are standing in a space that they know very well on all sides; they do not understand what it means to talk about the left side of the space, or about objects that occupy that space, and react as if they were partially blind, and they cannot be taught what the "left side" means. This is very different from real blindness, for someone who is blind knows there is a left side and a right side. Or some patients may recognize a given person or place but declare that it seems "alien" or "unreal"; there is something false or untrue, they say, about the recollection or recognition. No amount of insistence will convince them that what they are seeing is "real."

There is, then, a profound difference between normal and pathological recognition and remembering. Memory loss in the brain-damaged patient is not the loss of an "image" or a "memory trace" in the brain but rather evidence of a restructuring of the patient's conscious knowledge, a restructuring of the patient's relation to his or her surroundings. The brain has mechanisms for establishing this relation—that is the ultimate significance of the pathological evidence—and the most important consequence of these mechanisms is consciousness. With brain damage, function is altered, certain brain processes are no longer possible, and consequently consciousness, too, is altered. Gall was right to emphasize the problem of function, and though he did not fully grasp the implications of this, it suggests a radically different way of interpreting the clinical evidence. How we acquire a memory, the process of memory, and how our brains make the memories available for conscious or unconscious acts and thoughts— these are integral parts of memory itself. By suggesting that memory is separate from function, Wernicke may have falsified our understanding of numerous clinical disorders and of brain function in general. Recently, function has once again become an issue in neurological and scientific discussions of the brain, but unfortunately function has simply been added to models of the brain in which Wernicke's assumptions about memory are taken for granted.

Wernicke's views, not Gall's, came to dominate neurology. His is part of the classical school of neurological thought, and it remains dominant today.[8] Scientists for generations have searched for where and how memories are stored. By the end of the nineteenth century, it was known that the brain consisted of an enormous network of interconnected cells (some thirty billion), or neurons, and it was further recognized that neurons communicated with each other across a tiny gap called a synapse. In 1921 the Austrian physiologist Otto Loewi (1873–1961), inspired by a dream, discovered that transmission across the synapse is chemical: active neurons release a chemical substance called a neurotransmitter, which excites, in turn, the neighboring neuron. When neurons are active, the synaptic junctions tend to change; active synapses tend to be "strengthened," releasing more neurotransmitter into the synaptic gap. While these changes are related to the mechanisms of memory, there is no evidence that they represent any specific information being stored for later recall. To date, no one has been able to locate a specific memory in any part of the brain.

Nonetheless, the idea that the brain stores specific information that can be manipulated by separate functional units received support when in the late 1950s John von Neumann, the Hungarian-born mathematician and pioneer in computer development, suggested that the brain functions like a computer; certain regions of the brain are equivalent to specialized preprogrammed units in computers. Scientists in the field that came to be called artificial intelligence tried to unravel the details of these hypothetical programs and to build machines that might imitate various brain functions, such as seeing. Neurophysiological discoveries—most important among them David Hubel and Torsten Wiesel's findings that individual neurons in the brain were sensitive to lines and bars with specific horizontal, vertical, and oblique orientations—appeared to justify this line of computer research. At the same time, advances in medical technology permitted observation of the functioning of living brains; again, the evidence appeared to support the broad outlines of the new research programs. Neurophysiology, neurology, and artificial intelligence became parts of a grand synthesis—cognitive science, one of the most active and perhaps most promising "new" sciences of our day. Cognitive science is Franz Gall's greatest legacy, for the work of Gall and other nineteenth-century neurologists dominates its philosophical and psychological outlook. Yet in one sense cognitive science has eliminated Gall's implicit concern with consciousness, a twist in the fate of his doctrine that we owe to Carl Wernicke.

These ideas, however, have not always reigned uncontested. In the nineteenth century, the French physician Pierre Flourens (1794–1867) opposed Gall's views, arguing that the brain functions as a whole. But "holism," as this argument came to be known, lost its appeal after Broca's "discovery" of the "speech center," partly because the holists failed to explain what the various apparently specialized units of the brain had in common: in what ways the functional principles of the brain might be the same whether the brain was presented with visual, auditory, or other stimuli. The holistic view of the brain held that the functional principles (which were not specified) were the same in all parts of the brain and that the brain was a dynamic structure whose parts were not independently specialized but interdependent, acquiring specialized functions through experience. The clinical evidence overwhelmed this holistic viewpoint, and the holists had no evidence to explain what the different parts of the brain were doing and how they had acquired their special functions.

By the beginning of the twentieth century, some neurologists argued that the clinical evidence had been misunderstood. Gall's mistake had been to assume not that there are different mental faculties but that they are innately determined and have specific anatomical localizations in the brain. Different faculties emerge, they argued, through experience, and become organized within the brain in relatively similar ways from individual to individual. This seems obvious: various faculties, like speaking, recognizing faces, making certain motions, and so on, are grossly similar among all of us. After all, the general plan of our bodies and our brains is genetically determined, we live in the same world, and we communicate with each other and in a very general way confront similar problems. If Broca's and Wernicke's areas were in any sense localized brain functions—specialized organs of speech, say—it was their connections to the vocal apparatus and to the organs of hearing (and to other parts of the brain in which specific functions were developing as well) that made them appear predetermined or innate, not any innately determined internal structure or neuronal connectivity specific to the function of speech. (In fact, clinically, the localizations did not have the precision Broca or Wernicke had suggested, and the latter had in any case spoken only of localized memories, not of functions.)

But, then, if brain functions were not predetermined, how were they acquired? What does the brain do, and why does it eventually appear to perform quite specific functions? The answer that began to emerge at the beginning of this century criticized the classical clinical studies for ignoring a patient's "psychological" attributes, his or her state of consciousness. One of the principal proponents of the anticlassical view, the German neurologist Kurt Goldstein, described how a certain patient's behavior, and his failure to understand his own state of agitation, suggested that much had been overlooked:

> Here is a man with a lesion of the frontal lobe, to whom we present a problem in simple arithmetic. He is unable to solve it. But simply noting and recording the fact that he is unable to perform a simple multiplication would be an exceedingly inadequate account of the patient's reaction. Just looking at him, we can see a great deal more than this arithmetical failure. He looks dazed, changes color, becomes agitated, anxious, starts to fumble,his pulse becomes irregular; a moment before amiable, he is now sullen, evasive, exhibits temper, or even becomes aggressive. It takes some time before it is possible to continue the examination. Because the patient is so disturbed in his whole behavior, we call situations of this kind *catastrophic situations*.
>
> In the face of a task which he can perform, the same patient behaves in the opposite way. He looks animated and pleased, is steady and collected, interested, cooperative; he is "all there." One might infer from this contrast in behavior that the patient's reaction as a whole is simply his reaction to his experiencing adequacy or inadequacy, respectively, to the task. *But the fact that the reaction complex does not follow the performance or nonperformance, but occurs simultaneously with it, speaks against such an explanation. A further argument against it is that often the patients have no idea why they have been agitated, angry, or resistant.*
>
> As a matter of fact, the contrasting behavior is to be regarded as a manifestation of the capacity of the organism as a whole for success or failure in a task set for it.[9]

At the heart of Goldstein's view is the idea that the nature of memory had been misunderstood. Memory is not a precise reproducible entity, he argued, and if we are to understand it, we must understand how defects of memory are related to the patient's conscious reactions to his or her loss; memory, function, and consciousness are intimately related. This idea, I have suggested, was also implicit in Gall's work. But the defenders of the new view denied Gall's claim that functions are innate. Gall's views were profoundly revised, Wernicke's were rejected, and new clinical studies, clarifying the nature of memory, suggested an answer to the more general question about why specific functions, though not innate, emerged in all individuals. Recent developments in the neurosciences have made these ideas compelling.

It is one of the goals of this book to clarify and to make explicit the often implicit assumptions in these challenges to classical neurology and to note how contemporary developments in neurophysiology add powerful new arguments in their favor. Central to my thesis is the claim that the subjectivity of knowledge—my awareness that my thoughts, memories, and associated feelings are mine and while I can try to describe them I can never really communicate them to you—is created by neurological mechanisms whose existence clinical studies have clarified but that scientists and neurologists alike have overlooked to this day. Many features that once could not be understood in the clinical studies become less mysterious when one recognizes them as alterations and breakdowns in the mechanisms of subjectivity.

The first vague outlines of this argument were suggested in the beginning of the century when Kurt Goldstein and his colleague Adhémar Gelb reexamined the nature of memory loss following brain damage. In 1925 they published a study of a patient with brain damage who was able to distinguish colors but was unable to name them. Classical neurology could have easily explained the patient's difficulties as the result of damage to the memory traces of the names of colors. Goldstein rejected this explanation, for while his patient was able to match identical colors—for example, identical reds, or identical blues—he was unable to relate different shades of red or of green as belonging in the same group. Names, Goldstein argued, were abstractions, and a name such as "red" described a range of colors belonging to an abstract category. Goldstein thought his patient's difficulty was that he could not understand that the various shades of red all belonged to one category and therefore had the same name—he had lost the capacity to understand the name "red." Classical neurology could not explain how these categories, which are not innate or predetermined before birth, might have been created by the brain. And, more importantly, it could not explain—indeed, it ignored—why brain damage usually destroyed what Goldstein called "abstract" or "categorical" knowledge and left "concrete" knowledge intact; a patient might not be able to recognize various shades of red as all examples of the same color (a loss of categorical knowledge) but have no difficulty identifying a tie as "my red tie" (concrete knowledge). Clearly it was not memory that was at fault here; rather, the patient's understanding of the world had been restructured. Yet Goldstein's critique is largely ignored today, and cognitive science has come to the defense of the classical view.

The same failure of "classical" neurology is apparent in the Soviet neurologist Alexandr Luria's case of a man with an extraordinary memory, made famous in his *The Mind of a Mnemonist*. Unable to lead an ordinary life, Luria's mnemonist spent his days exhibiting his extraordinary memory in public performances: lists of words, often without meaning, lists of telephone numbers or names, were read off to him, and moments later he could faultlessly repeat them. The mnemonist explained that he used various tricks to accomplish these feats; for example, he would create a mental map of his daily walks in the city and place the cited words and numbers in front of different landmarks or buildings that he knew well. But he had a very limited repertoire of such memory tricks; he had, indeed, a very poor memory. He could organize and abstract the facts of his experience and the world around him only by using his tricks. A truly good memory requires, on the contrary, a capacity to organize experience in many different ways.

In fact, though neither he nor Luria was aware of it, the mnemonist was using techniques that were not new. Since the time of ancient Greece, there were well-known "memory arts" by which people had been taught to place images in ordered arrangements in the "spaces of the mind." Practitioners of these arts of memory were concerned with creating new ideas and images as much as with remembering old ones. After the invention of printing, they often modeled their work on the idea of a printed page on which a few symbols—the letters of the alphabet, say—could be arranged in space to create all the words in a language. So, too, mastering the art of memory permitted its practitioner to create new ideas, new poetry, through its subtle combinatory logic. But it was these combinatory skills that the mnemonist lacked; he relied on retracing the monotonous paths of his daily walks, and thus the limitation of his memory. The art of memory was a technique, a process, for recalling old images as well as creating new ones; implicitly, its inventors had understood that memory is creative and dynamic.[10]

Like Goldstein's patient, Luria's mnemonist could not generalize. He understood colors only in relation to specific objects: "When I hear the word *green*, a green flowerpot appears; with the word *red* I see a man in a red shirt coming towards me. . . . Even numbers remind me of images. Take the number 1. This is a proud well-built man. . . ." Further-more, extraneous noises produced "blurs," "splashes," or "puffs of steam" that confused the mnemonist's visual images: "You see, every sound bothers me . . . it's transformed into a line and becomes confusion. . . . Other times smoke or fog appears . . . and the more people talk, the harder it gets, until I reach a point where I can't make anything out."[11] The meaning of words became confused, his responses verbose, irrelevant, and even rude.

An apparently unrelated syndrome was described by the French neurologist Gilles de la Tourette in 1885. Tourette's syndrome, as the affliction is today known, is characterized by sudden brief spasms of uncoordinated movements, usually followed by grunting sounds that in more developed forms of the disease are transformed into a repetition of words and bits of sentences. These repetitions are frequently punctuated by verbal obscenities:

Most of the time, when the convulsion of uncoordinated movements is at its peak, the patient utters an inarticulate cry that is often difficult to translate, a *hem, ouh, oah, ah,* that always in relation with the uncoordinated movements can be uttered several times in a row and at different times in the course of the day. When this inarticulate cry exists, it can change into a characteristically *articulate* cry of a word that is often an echo (or repetition of a word the patient has just heard).

The repetition of a word or phrase suggests an attempt to overcome an *inability to understand* it:

All the patient's intellectual faculties are momentarily con-centrated on this word or phrase; his preoccupation is such that he can lose the thread of the speaker's words, or of the matter he is reading. The patient tends to repeat aloud this word, be it one he has just heard or one he has just read, always at the moment of his muscular spasms or just as they terminate.[12]

Just as an "extraneous" noise caused "blurs" or "puffs of steam" in the memory images of Luria's mnemonist, making it impossible for him to make sense of the memory image, an extraneous noise or flash of light confuses the patient with Tourette's syndrome, and then he cannot make sense of what he is hearing or reading. He desperately tries to seize its meaning by repeating the word or phrase. Tourette described the pathetic and absurd consequences of these futile efforts:

> One evening in 1883, Mademoiselle X was undressing for bed when a dog began barking under her bedroom window. She immediately began involuntarily imitating the dog's barking. She was unable to fall asleep until one o'clock in the morning, because her body was constantly racked by muscular spasms accompanied by a loud barking sound much like that of the dog.
> Another curious observation:
> Mademoiselle X had a marked tendency to imitate others' gestures or bizarre positions that had struck her. One day she was walking with her teacher on a fairgrounds. She saw a cardboard Gargantua whose mouth opened and closed in a regular manner, gobbling up anything that was placed in it. The child studied this sight with astonishment; for the rest of her promenade she ceaselessly opened and closed her mouth involuntarily, just as the Gargantua had.[13]

The Touretter fails to understand not only linguistic signs but often the actions of others, which he repeats (in an effort at understanding) with sometimes tragic consequences. As Tourette reported:

> One day the steamer's cook (with Tourette's syndrome) was standing on the bridge of the ship and cradling a child in his arms when a sailor appeared and, in the manner of the cook, cradled a block of wood in his arms. The sailor then threw the block on an awning and amused himself making it roll around the awning cloth. The cook immediately imitated him with the child. The sailor then released the awning and the wood fell on the bridge of the ship; the cook did likewise, and the little boy was instantly killed.[14]

The Touretter's tics, gesticulations, and imitations hint at a deep connection between understanding (consciousness) and body movement—ultimately, as I will discuss in later chapters, between understanding and body image. Understanding—like memory, which is essential to understanding—is always achieved from a particular vantage point or frame of reference; my recollections are in terms of my life, yours are in terms of your life. The reason we understand experience in terms of what *we* can do is that our brains automatically relate the actions to ourselves. Imitation is the Touretter's way of trying to give meaning to observed actions by establishing the body as the frame of reference.

Since the frame of reference (the body image) is dynamic, understanding, too, is dynamic. Neurological problems severely limit the range and dynamic qualities of the body image, and one consequence may be the emergence of what are called "multiple personalities," when the dynamic quality of the body-image frame of reference is partly destroyed and the normal subtle sliding from one personality to another, which we all experience to some slight degree in normal life, is replaced by a severe "jumping" among personalities in a limited repertoire. The intimate connections among memory, body image, frame of reference, and understanding can be seen in the case of Luria's mnemonist, who appeared to have just such a "split" in his personality. He attributed his rude behavior to another self, which he could not control: "I'm sitting in your apartment preoccupied with my own thoughts. You, being a good host, ask: 'How do you like these cigarettes?' 'So-so, fair . . .' That is, I'd never say that, but 'he' says things he ought not to."[15] The other self, the "he," was responsible for most of the mnemonist's actions: "I had to go to school. . . . I saw myself here, while 'he' was to go off to school. I'm angry with 'him'—why is he taking so long to get ready?"[16]

Like Luria's mnemonist, patients with Tourette's syndrome manifest a momentary inability to synthesize or abstract stimuli; the mnemonist complains of "blurs" and "puffs of steam" and talks profusely, incoherently, and even rudely; the Touretter desperately imitates and ultimately curses. Touretter and mnemonist become stuck on a detail—a word, a sound—that "blocks out" other stimuli. Like Goldstein's patient, they cannot understand that different shades of red are all examples of "red"; they can see the individual reds but not how they are related. Goldstein's, Luria's, and Tourette's patients all have profoundly altered awarenesses of the world and, consequently, profoundly altered personalities. As one Touretter said, "You 'normals' . . . have all feelings, all styles, available all the time—gravity, levity, whatever is appropriate. We Touretters don't. . . . *You* are free, you have a natural balance, we must make the best of an artificial balance."[17]

Unlike these patients, ordinary people can normally expand their awareness and establish subtle new relationships. Whenever we suddenly achieve an understanding—as for example, in reading a murder mystery, when a vital clue that we have overlooked takes on a new and compelling importance—we are aware of something that escaped our attention before; we see an object or a person in new terms. What we suddenly "see" or "understand" is a new thing, neither the person or object as it was a few moments earlier, nor the change in either, but a fusion of the two. Consciousness, understanding, has been transformed—the realization of changes in an old friend, the recognition of the importance of a clue, the perception of hitherto unseen forms in a drawing, or even the sudden sense of familiarity as we walk along a city street. In all these cases, our consciousness of the street, the drawing, the friend, the mystery plot, is made up neither of the new image alone nor of the old one, but of the relation between the two and our "conscious" sense of both. All thoughts, all conscious images, are a mixing of the old and the new, creations that are neither one nor the other.

Consciousness is a state of awareness. Most animals probably feel conscious, but unlike human beings, who have language, they are not self-aware, or "conscious of being conscious"; they ignore their own image in a mirror. No one has been able to explain the physiological basis of self-awareness, but numerous clinical studies have shown that human states of awareness can be profoundly altered by brain damage. Indeed, unless one accounts for consciousness, most if not all clinical work on brain-damaged patients becomes virtually impossible to understand. Patients with brain damage are confused when they fail to recognize and remember, and it is this confused, altered awareness, as much as any specific failures of memory, that is symptomatic of their illness.

Recognition and remembering are conscious acts, and failures of memory consequent upon brain damage are not due to the loss of specific items "stored" somewhere in the brain but to a breakdown of the mechanisms of consciousness. A patient's state of confusion is no more to be ignored than his failure to recognize, say, his home. Memory, recognition, and consciousness are all part of the same process. And while the physiological mechanisms may largely, but not completely, elude us, intriguing discoveries and ideas nonetheless suggest a new and exciting view of consciousness, however incomplete and sketchy. We now know enough to reinterpret much that classical neurology taught us. Recent developments in neurophysiology and new theoretical work are beginning to suggest a view that will account for human psychology with a richness that the dominant theories of our day have generally not allowed. A new synthesis is emerging that must, I believe, profoundly alter our understanding of psychology, philosophy, and the nature and basis of language. One challenge to the classical view is the phenomenon of the "alien" limb, for here the breakdown of conscious mechanisms is clearly an unavoidable issue. Neurologists and psychologists have to this day ignored it, as we shall see in the following chapter.

II

The Counterfeit Leg and the Bankruptcy
of Classical Neurology

In 1745 Julien Offroy de La Mettrie (1709–1751) scandalized
Europe when he suggested, in his *Histoire naturelle de l'âme*
(Natural History of the Soul), that the soul was a superfluous
idea, and that Descartes had written of it only to keep the
priests happy. The French Parliament voted that the book be
burned, and La Mettrie was dismissed from his position as
physician to the French Guard. He took refuge in Holland.
There he anonymously published his *L'Homme machine* in
1747, but its fate was hardly better. The Dutch government
ordered the destruction of the book and began an extensive
search for its author. Frederick II of Prussia invited La Mettrie
to Berlin, where he spent the rest of his brief life. "Thought
is a property of matter," La Mettrie wrote in his scandalous
book. "All ideas come from the senses," and they are produced
by the brain: "If the brain is both well organized and well
trained, then it is like rich earth well sowed, which produces
a hundredfold of what it received."[1]

It was Franz Gall who, in his own writings, captured the
dynamic and creative character of the brain suggested in La
Mettrie's work. But others in the eighteenth century stressed

La Mettrie's view that knowledge originated in the senses; they drew inspiration from the English philosopher John Locke (1632–1704) as well: sense data was stored in the brain as "representative images," as Gall put it; the brain created associations among these images, and the associated images were "thoughts."

A century later, it was possible for Carl Wernicke to apply this view—that thought was the association of elementary sensations—to neurology without risk of scandal. Neurologists applauded his simple, elegant model of speech and understanding. For example, according to him, the auditory sensations of words, which were stored as memory images in one part of the brain, could be associated with their spoken forms, which elsewhere in the brain were stored as memory images of the sensations of lip and tongue movements, by nerve fibers that ran from one area to the other. In the following years, "diagrams" of the brain's associational powers became commonplace: specialized memory centers for different kinds of sensations were shown with a variety of interconnections. Neurological symptoms were explained as being the consequence of the destruction of a memory center for a particular kind of sensation or of one of the connecting pathways.

All these models, however, were based on a static view of the information the brain was storing. The diagram makers were not troubled, for example, by the fact that many words sound the same but have very different meanings (in English, for example, "hare" and "hair"). When speaking a language normally, of course, we recognize the intended meaning of a sound from the context, the sentence, or the circumstances in which it is spoken. But different speakers pronounce words differently, and a given speaker may pronounce the same word in a number of different ways. The neurologists were not clear as to just what the nature of a specific "auditory-word-memory image" was or how it was acquired. Nor were they clear on why some "images" were stored and others not. In fact, it was unclear how any stored auditory memory image could be used for recognition of a word unless one argued that subsequent encounters with the word (or object) were identical to the initial encounter, which created the memory image. The truth is, "stored" knowledge has to be dynamic if recognition is to be possible, but the diagram makers seemed little troubled by this problem. Their success in explaining neurological disorders of language had been spectacular.

And yet that very success was peculiar. For though they had been concerned with language, they had not addressed themselves to issues of "meaning," "understanding," or even "consciousness" and the relation of these to memory. Neither philosophy nor psychology had anything to do with their models, though it is difficult to imagine how they could be avoided in any discussion of language, however abstract.

But if the neurologists successfully avoided these issues in their discussions of linguistic disorders, they could hardly ignore them when they came to describing cases in which patients lost awareness of their bodies. Diagrams failed. Neurologists were mystified, and they remain so to this day. If we think in terms other than theirs, we can see now that these cases, as they recorded them, suggest some deep connections between memory, understanding and consciousness.

In 1905 the French neurologists G. Deny and P. Camus published one of the earliest studies of a patient who had lost body awareness.[2] Their patient, Madame I, was a twenty-eight-year-old woman with a history of frequent emotional outbursts, who often wept without provocation. She attributed her difficulties to the violent character of her husband. Following one of her frequent disputes with him, she was interned in the Salpêtrière Hospital in Paris. She had been there for two years when Deny and Camus published their report.

Her illness began with a period of mental confusion. She became forgetful, wandered about, and undressed herself in the middle of the street. On several occasions she attempted suicide.

When her state of confusion passed, Madame I described what she called her "general insensibility":

> I'm no longer aware of myself as I used to be. I can no longer feel my arms, my legs, my head, and my hair. I have to touch myself constantly in order to know how I am. I have the feeling that my entire body is changed, even at times that it no longer exists. I touch an object, but it is not I who am touching it. I no longer feel as I used to. I cannot find myself. I cannot imagine myself. My insensibility is frightening, as if everything were empty.

Her clothes unbuttoned, she constantly touched herself, as she said, incessantly rubbed her naked skin, pulled at her hair, or scratched her head as she spoke. She was insensitive to cold. In bed she didn't know where her legs were unless she touched them or rubbed one against the other. "I don't know how I lie in my bed. I am always looking for my body and my legs; and in the morning I ask myself what happened during the night." When her mouth was closed she could not find her tongue because she thought it was in her throat.

Taste and smell were gone; she was never hungry; voices and the sounds of the street were no longer the same. Things looked different:

> The world appears changed to me. People and things appear like phantoms, as if they are not real. I recognize

them, but they no longer seem the same. When my husband and children come to visit me, they don't appear to be as real as they once were. I recognize them, but seeing them doesn't give me any pleasure. I don't experience anything, I am insensitive to everything. It is terrible to be like this. I don't love anyone, and I can't even love myself. Life means nothing to me. I'd rather die.

Nor could she remember what she had once known well: "I can imagine neither my parents, nor the interior of my house, nor other places that I know well. I have forgotten the tastes of food, the odor of flowers, and the voices of my children. Sensations never remain with me, and I can never recall them."

Physically her head often felt heavy and her throat tight. She had difficulty in breathing and was often thirsty, "but after drinking I don't feel that I have had anything to drink." None of this troubled her; it was her "insensibility" that made her suffer and complain. Deny and Camus wrote:

Though she is profoundly handicapped by her state, Madame I is perfectly clearheaded. She tries to analyze her problems without wild interpretations or hysterical ideas. At moments when she is not dominated by her anxiety, she helps other patients, reads, and sews. But most of the time she tries to recover her lost sensibility. And her complaint is always the same: "I don't feel and see myself as I used to; when I speak I no longer hear the sound of my own voice. I don't feel that I am doing things. I no longer have the desire to eat, for I seem to be incapable of feeling hungry. I am insensitive everywhere; it is as if I were dead."

Physical examination revealed that Madame I had normal sensitivity to touch, that she could distinguish hot from cold, and that she could identify objects by touch with her eyes closed. Her sense of smell and taste were normal, and her vision was slightly disturbed only in judging distance.

What was not normal was her failure to recognize the position of her arms and legs, and her complete insensitivity to pain. When her skin was pierced with a needle, she showed no signs of discomfort, though the sight of a cauterizing instrument frightened her. Deny and Camus ended their account with these words:

> Since her admission, the patient has remained in the same state. Constantly she says that she cannot feel the different parts of her body, that she does not have the same sense of her surroundings as in the past, and that she is incapable of normal recall of the images that are stored in her memory. She claims that she is lost, that her disease is incurable and she will never get better; she accepts neither treatment nor consolation.

In their desperation and in their need to touch, there were superficial resemblances between Madame I and Cheselden's young boy who recovered his sight. A thousand times a day he called a cat a "dog," touched it, and then corrected himself: he was sure he knew only when he could touch. And Madame I was desperately seeking to know that she *was* herself by touching her own flesh. She was trying to create a self, assure herself of her own existence. Cheselden's patient knew he existed; Madame I did not, and failing to establish her existence, she could not remember her past. She could not imagine ("represent to myself") her parents, her house, and other places and people she had known well.

Madame I's case shows, I believe, that there are no memories without a sense of self. Without knowledge of one's own being, one can have no recollections. How can I remember *my* parents, *my* house, if I am not sure *I* exist? We must not overlook the essential nature of all human (and perhaps some animal) memories: *Every recollection refers not only to the remembered event or person or object but to the person who is remembering.* The very essence of memory is subjective, not mechanical reproduction; and essential to that subjective psychology is that every remembered image of a person, place, idea, or object inevitably contains, whether explicitly or implicitly, a basic reference to the person who is remembering. Madame I was desperately trying to recreate that reference to herself by touching her body, since she could not otherwise remember her past. Unable to know her body as part of her memory (her brain could not create a body image), she could not imagine, or recreate in her mind, images of her parents or the houses where she had lived. Madame I's existence was in doubt to her own self, and hence so, too, were her memories. Her attempt to create a sense of self, her constant touching and rubbing of her own body, is a metaphor for memory; a brain isolated from the body has no memory.

Madame I succeeded in creating momentary images of herself as she ran her hands through her hair and over her body. And during those moments she could recognize her husband and children too. But the images were disconnected, referring neither to one another nor, as a consequence, to a continuous image of herself, and hence they were phantom-like. Her body existed only intermittently, in starts and stops; and so did her recognitions. What changed in her sense of taste, in her hearing the voices of people she knew or seeing them before her, was not that these sensations no longer matched various stored images (as the classical neurologist would have it) but that they lacked the normal continuity in time they once had had. She could re-create momentary images only when she was verifying to herself that she had a body.

Thus her brain was not comparing her sensations to stored images and telling her that what she was seeing or smelling had "changed." No, her brain was creating a series of disconnected images that, though familiar, lacked a continuous point of reference (her body, her self) and hence a temporal flow, a continuity in time. What she called a "change" in her body was in fact a loss of a sense of bodily continuity, a temporal link between sensations from moment to moment; and she desperately tried to create this as she ran her hands over her limbs. She had an abstract knowledge of the flow of time, and through language she could instinctively know something was missing, something had "changed" in the world around her. But language could not restore the continuity of sensory images, their "meaning," and hence their familiarity; for that she needed a sense of her own body. She recognized her parents and children, but they were unfamiliar and she was unmoved by them; they had lost all meaning for her.

Deny and Camus believed that Madame I's loss of her body image and the unreality of her recollections—her husband and children appearing less "real than they once were"—were not interrelated problems; for them, both had the same root cause—a failure to integrate, to associate, sensations that formed the body image or the recollection:

> If it is admitted with Wernicke that awareness of our corporeal existence is entirely subordinated to the integrity of the organic sensations transmitted to the brain at each moment from every part of the body . . . it is evident that the suppression, or nonutilization, by the conscious of one category of organic sensations (visceral, muscular, articular, etc.) will suffice to create a more or less profound perturbation, which may give rise to a simple doubt or the complete denial of our bodily existence.

And so, too, Deny and Camus attributed the unreality of Madame I's recollections to the failure to transmit to the brain one or another sensation; the loss of a sensation "normally associated with our sensorial perceptions" could, they believed, provoke "the same perplexity, the same doubts, the same negative tendencies concerning the exterior world."

But such doubts imply that one *knows* there is something missing. How can one know a sensation is missing if it is not "transmitted" or is suppressed? What is the brain's frame of reference that creates such doubts? Deny and Camus imply that the brain both knows (unconsciously) and yet does not know (consciously), and because of the ambiguity, one doubts the existence of one's body or of another person. But Madame I doubted her own existence, and it was her inability to establish a sense of self that lay at the root of her doubts about the existence of others. When we doubt that something (or someone) is familiar, we cannot establish with certainty its relation to ourselves. Madame I, lacking a body image, could not establish this relationship, and hence her sense of the unfamiliarity of the familiar drove her to run her hands so desperately over her body. Curiously, Deny and Camus remain silent about her constant need to touch herself.

Another French neurologist, Pierre Bonnier, rejected their train of thought without, however, explicit reference to this issue, and came closer to understanding the problem. Bonnier had in 1893 written a study of vertigo, in which he had argued that it was due to a loss of the sense of space.[3] The notion of space, he had argued, permitted the brain to give meaning to all sensory experience: "The only concrete quality, the only objective property, that we can sensorily attribute to matter is to be *somewhere* [*quelque part*] and consequently *something* [*quelque chose*]." To him, the notion of an object is *always* associated with the notion of space. Hence, Bonnier concluded, the sense of space must be absolute. Madame I had lost it.

But this still failed to answer what Madame I was doing when she ran her hands over her body. The deeper clue that Bonnier, like Deny and Camus, overlooked was Madame I's loss of pain. The sense of pain is a consequence of brain mechanisms that establish awareness of the existence of the body; the body, not a sense of absolute space, is the brain's absolute frame of reference. Sensations, as Bonnier rightly noted, would not be possible without a frame of reference; nor would memories. All sensations (cold/hot, rough/smooth) are relational or relative; so, too, are memories. The brain establishes relations, and the primary one is the object's relation to the individual: self-reference. It was a breakdown in this self-reference that destroyed Madame I's body image (the relation between her body as object and her self) and made her recollections unfamiliar. In running her hands over her body, she was trying to establish the human being's most basic frame of reference. That human memory always has this bodily self-aware frame of reference is what makes it so different from any image-retaining capability in a machine.*

Bonnier's challenge to the diagram makers was but one of many such challenges at the beginning of this century. There was a pervasive sense that observed psychological changes in certain patients were little accounted for by the diagram makers' anatomical descriptions. It is no accident that Sigmund Freud attacked the diagram makers in his book *On Aphasia* in 1891 and then abandoned neurology for the rest of his life. Psychoanalytic theory denies that there is an exact replica of conscious memories in unconscious form. At the heart of the theory is the idea that an individual's reaction to his or her own memories—whether denial of their validity, "inappropri-

---

*Madame I may have had a lesion in her limbic system, a part of the brain that was first described by Paul Broca in 1878 and that by the 1930s was shown to be associated with emotions. See pages 85–6.

ate'' indifference to painful recollections, or inaccurate re-creation of them—reveals much about the workings of the mind. It was an insight not unrelated to Bonnier's idea that objects were knowable only in terms of space. Both views insist that knowledge requires a frame of reference, though, for sure, Freud's was far deeper and more interesting. He recognized not only that memories are self-referential (though he did not explicitly discuss this notion) but that the nature of self-reference is complex and often difficult to discern. Indeed, for Freud all *individual* knowledge is self-referential. We understand the story of Oedipus, for example, because we hear it as being about ourselves. He was certainly right about that; our question here must be, however, what is the nature of the self to which reference is made?

Classical neurology was never troubled with a patient's attitude, response, or reaction to his or her own thoughts. And if some neurologists, at the turn of the century, found Freud's work unenlightening, they nonetheless recognized that a patient's way of talking about memories could not be ignored. Associationist models made by the diagram makers predicted nothing about a patient's reactions to his or her own memories—or to any inability to remember. Indeed, the diagram makers' idea of memory as a group of associations—the sight of a word being associated with a sound and with an image of the object it refers to, for example—could not account for the transformations of memories, could not account for the way we construct new memories out of old memories.

The English neurologist Henry Head noted that in strictly neurological terms, brain activity at any moment is not an isolated event but is related to what the brain has been doing just before: it is ''a march of events with a definite temporal relation; the response obtained from any one point, at a particular moment, depends on what has happened before.'' Head's neurology was in the same spirit as Freud's psychology; the past and the present are intimately intertwined in subtle ways that reveal neither one nor the other directly but that constitute both. Recognition, Head noted in 1920, requires a series of images, none of which is precisely the "image" of which one is aware.

The idea of body posture, for example, is not absolute but relational. When we describe someone as sitting "upright" or standing "erect," we are inevitably implying a distinction from postures that might be slouched or slightly bent. If all humans always carried themselves stiffly upright, the observation would be unnecessary and the term meaningless. In fact, since we constantly change the positions of our bodies, it is obvious that our descriptions of body posture at particular moments will be relational. It would be impossible, Head argued, to discover the position of any part of "the body, unless the immediate postural sensations were related to something that had preceded them. A direct perception of posture, analogous to that of roughness, is impossible; in every case the new position of the limb is relative to some previous posture."[*][4]

Perception of posture, then, is no more an isolated perception than a single fingerprint can be a helpful clue in a murder case without a body in time and space to which it can be related. The very idea of posture is of a relation between the body's present and immediately preceding positions, just as a fingerprint is a clue in relation to other, previously discovered clues. Perception of an immediate sensation is possible only in relation to a preceding one, and the latter, too, makes sense only in relation to earlier ones, and so on *ad infinitum*. Head's analysis suggests that we can never really "know" our own

---

[*] Roughness, too, is relational. Head was wrong to assume otherwise.

posture. In a murder case, a fingerprint is one of a limited number of clues referring to a murder victim, but there is virtually no limit to the movements and positions the body can assume, just as there is virtually no limit to the number of sensations one can experience. Of course, we can avoid the infinite regress of Head's argument, as many scientists and philosophers have done, by assuming that knowledge is determined by innate programs that create images directly knowable by the brain, images that form the basis of subsequent recognitions. But this does not explain the subjectivity of knowledge, my sense that what I see and know is my exclusive knowledge, which I may be able to talk about but you will never feel and understand as I do.

Freud tried to account for the highly individual ways in which similar perceptions are understood and acted upon. He avoided an infinite regress (when I see Jane, I am really thinking of Mary, who in turn reminds me of Janet, and so on) by postulating that the Oedipus complex (and the person's relation to the father and mother) was the ultimate point of reference. Head's formulation lacks such an ultimate point of reference, and yet, implicitly at least, it suggests that the body image is the brain's frame of reference:

Every recognisable change enters into consciousness already charged with its relation to something that has gone before, just as on a taxi meter the distance is presented to us already transformed into shillings and pence. So the final product of the tests for the appreciation of posture or passive movement rises into consciousness as a measured postural change.

For this combined standard, against which all subsequent changes of posture are measured before they enter consciousness, we propose the word "schema." By means of perpetual alterations in position we are always building up a postural model of ourselves which constantly changes. Every new posture of movement is recorded on this plastic schema, and the activity of the cortex brings every fresh group of sensations evoked by altered posture into relation with it. Immediate postural recognition follows as soon as the relation is complete.[5]

With the body image as a frame of reference, the relation of "immediate postural sensations" to "something that had preceded them" does not give rise to an infinite regress of points of reference. And the brain's point of view is unique. The richness of each subjective world is thus a consequence of the dynamic qualities of the person's body image, which the brain uses as a frame of reference. Consciousness is a "happening": "This is the case with all the higher projectional aspects of sensation; they form a continuous series of dispositions, determined by previous events of a like order. The unit of consciousness, as far as these factors in sensation are concerned, is not a moment of time, but a 'happening'."[6]

Thus the body image becomes conscious by reference to itself; it is its own frame of reference—"the immediate postural sensations were related to something that immediately preceded them." Recognition of anything must in general also have a frame of reference, and the only ever-present image to which the brain can always refer is that of the body. Through this ever-changing dynamic image the brain creates a conscious world of extraordinary variety, organizing stimuli dynamically in its terms. It is to this dynamic image that stimuli are referred (self-reference) and in terms of which they "make sense." The qualitative richness of each person's perceptual world is created by the dynamic qualities of his or her body image; without it there would be no world that anyone could know. When we grasp this fundamental nature of the brain's activity, we can see the enormous importance of our conscious and unconscious attempts to maintain and to create the body image. The Viennese neurologist and psychiatrist Paul Schilder (1886–1940) captured the dynamics of this struggle in the following passage:

> There are tendencies to make the body-image complete, but it cannot remain so without a renewed effort. There are opposite tendencies as well. There is a tendency towards the dissolution of the body-image. When we close our eyes and remain as motionless as possible, the body-image tends towards dissolution. The body-image is the result of an effort and cannot be completely maintained when the effort ceases. The body-image is, to put it in a paradoxical way, never a complete structure; it is never static: there are always disrupting tendencies. With the changing physiological situations of life new structuralizations have to take place, and the life situations are always changing.[7]

But what if there were a partial breakdown of the mechanisms by which the body image is referred to itself? What if the left arm, for example, loses self-reference? Would the body image become deformed? Would memories change too? Neurologists were puzzled when in 1914 the French physician M. J. Babinski reported to the Society of Neurology in Paris cases of patients who seemed unaware of their paralyzed arms or legs.[8] He described a woman who had become paralyzed on the left side of her body, had no memory loss, and, though intelligent and perfectly rational,

> appeared completely to ignore the existence of her paralyzed left side. She never complained; she never made any reference to her paralyzed left side. If she was asked to move her

right arm, she immediately carried out the request. Asked to move her left arm, she remained immobile, keeping silent and carrying on as if the question had been asked of someone else.

Another woman, similarly paralyzed on her left side, joked that her physician had always succeeded in curing her ailments but that this time "his science was impotent." She, too, readily moved her right arm when asked. When asked to do the same with her left arm, she either failed to respond or said, "There, it's done," as she remained perfectly immobile. When she overheard her physicians discussing the possibility of using electrotherapy on her paralyzed arm, she asked them why they wanted to do that: "For I'm not paralyzed." Another semi-paralyzed patient also did not move his left hand when asked; when told to look and see that his left arm had not moved, the patient was neither surprised nor particularly upset. "It's that it moves more slowly than the other," he said.

Other patients—the physician Oliver Sacks in our own day, for example—have reported on paralyzed legs or arms that "Looked and felt uncannily alien—a lifeless replica attached to my body. . . . It's just a counterfeit. It's not real. It's not mine." Sacks, who was personally afflicted with such a disorder, felt that it was *not just a lesion in my muscle, but a lesion in me.* He vividly described how the leg, *his* leg, past and present, disappeared:

The leg had vanished, taking its "place" with it. Thus there seemed no possibility of recovering it—and this irrespective of the pathology involved. Could memory help, where looking forward could not? No! The leg had vanished, taking its "past" away with it! I could no longer remember having a leg. I could no longer remember how I had ever walked and climbed. I felt inconceivably cut off from the person who had walked and run and climbed just five days before. There was only a "formal" continuity between us. There was a gap—an absolute gap—between then and now; and in that gap, into the void, the former "I" had vanished—the "I" who could thoughtlessly stand, run and walk, who was totally and thoughtlessly sure of his body, who couldn't conceive how doubts about it could possibly arise. . . . Into that gap, that void, outside space and time, the reality and possibilities of the leg had passed, and disappeared. I had often thought the phrase "vanished into the blue" at once absurd yet mysteriously significant. As if to rebuke my unbelief, my own leg had vanished "into the blue"; . . . I couldn't imagine it returning in any "normal" or physical way, because it had vanished from space and time—vanished, taking its space-and-time with it. . . . It had passed out of existence (whatever one meant by "existence"); and, by the same token, it would somehow have to come back *into* existence.[9]

Neurologists tried to explain these cases as they had the various language disorders they studied in brain-damaged patients (the aphasias)—without attending to the most fundamental problem, the nature of the self-awareness. J. Dejerine, a famous diagram maker, commented: "The patients of M. Babinski . . . have an altered sensibility of their paralyzed limbs. It is possible that this must be part of the reason for their indifference to their inability to act." And another neurologist, Henri Claude, commented: "It is possible that in the cases M. Babinski describes, there has been a loss of the representation of the paralyzed limb, and therefore the patient's attention is no longer drawn to it by motor and psycho-motor excitations."[10] More recently, it has been suggested that "if one treats perception and imagery as processes best described by a complex flow diagram, there may well be a number of different types of impairment, each of which manifests itself as neglect."[11]

Yet none of these patients actually complained of "altered sensibility." The leg is, rather, "alien," "counterfeit"; these are ways of describing an altered relationship between the leg and the self, for when a patient calls a leg "alien," he or she has a frame of (self-) reference, a sense of self, and knows the difference between "I" and "it." That is to say, the patient's unimpaired verbal and symbolic capabilities were attending to the limb and, in describing it, giving it a relational reality it would not otherwise have had. An injured dog or cow, which lacks verbal and symbol-making powers, would not have an "alien" limb, though it might *behave* as if its leg were alien; it simply "neglects" the leg, as the diagram makers imagined people did, being "indifferent" to it. If we cannot *describe* how something is related to us, it is not either "part" of us or "alien" to us. Sacks's leg, paralyzed and impervious to pain, did not feel like *his* leg, but he could see it; lacking the mechanism of self-reference, his brain could not make sense of what he was seeing; therefore the leg looked bizarre to him, or weird—and he called it "alien."

It is important to notice that seeing is not by itself "knowing" and that the lack of inner self-reference, together with the incontrovertible sight of the leg, therefore created a paradoxical relation to it. Sacks is conscious of his leg when he looks at it, and yet he cannot control its status—the nature of its relation to him—with this conscious visual image. A dog or cow, lacking symbolic thought, would not reflect on the status of a paralyzed leg; Sacks's verbal (symbolic) reflections establish a more abstract status for his leg than either a dog or cow could experience. Here we can see how language so profoundly alters the nature of consciousness.

Emotions, too, are part of the structure of self-reference. Sacks's altered awareness of his leg is an altered *emotional* relation to the leg as well; consciousness cannot be separated from emotion. One can have feelings for, one can love, only someone (or something) who has some sort of relation—be it indifferent, hostile, or loving—to oneself. Sacks is quite frightened by his paralyzed leg, but he does not have feelings about it; when it begins to recover sensation, in particular the sense of pain, it becomes a part of his self-referent system, and he regains his feelings about it.

> Back in my room, on my bed, I hugged the redeemed leg, or rather cast, though even this seemed living now, transfused with the life of the leg. "You dear old thing, you sweet thing," I found myself saying. "You've come back, you're real, you're part of me now." Its reality, its presence, its dearness, were all one. I gazed at it in a sort of bliss, filled with the sense of intense physicality. . . . I felt aflame with amazement, gratitude, joy—aflame with love, worship, praise. "Thank God," I cried, and "God be praised"— ejaculations, verbal forms, which suddenly had sense.[12]

The frightening initial blank in the emotional relation to a paralyzed limb reflects the breakdown of virtually all relations the brain can establish with it. However, the brain can still establish a visual relation, and this relation is inevitably ambiguous, or paradoxical, since all other evidence the brain has suggests that the limb does not exist. The peculiarity of this paradox is expressed in the patient's sense that the visual space, the place, that the leg occupies has disappeared. This partial loss of the sense of the leg's space, again, shows the centrality of self-reference: we sense space by its relation to something else, and essentially to our own bodies. Indeed, the disappearance of the place—the part of space—the leg occupies for the brain-damaged patient suggests that the brain creates our sense of space by reference to body image; the sense of self that gives the leg meaning creates meaning for the space it occupies as well. Body image is essential to our idea of space, and from an abstraction of it the brain derives more general notions of space and objects. Since the damaged brain—in the case of these patients—is unable to establish the relation between an alien limb and the body image, it cannot establish any sense of the space the limb would occupy either. As Bonnier so rightly noted, *something* must be *somewhere*.

The idea of space is, of course, abstract; it is a mental construct, a way of describing an aspect of the external world. What we mean or understand by the idea of space, then, emerges from self-reference; in cases of alien limbs, self-reference is destroyed and with it the idea of the space the limb occupies. Meaning and understanding are parts of the structure of consciousness that emerge from self-reference; they cannot exist without a body image. If all self-reference were destroyed, consciousness and understanding would not be possible.

For example, heaviness and lightness are comparative, relational ideas. A grand piano appears heavier than a teacup, and this idea of relative weights of objects ultimately derives from the relation between those objects and the body image. A patient with Parkinson's disease reported that when his body was not affected by the disease, a teacup felt "light" but that when his body became rigid, the teacup and everything around him appeared very "heavy." The idea of "lightness" (a bridge might appear to be floating in space) emerges from the brain's self-reference to the body image: a mobile (dynamic) body image gives the impression of a teacup as being "light;" a rigid body image gives the impression that a teacup or other objects in view are heavy. A sense of the weight and density of things is therefore intimately related to one's own bodily movements.

The disappearance of space or "place" in patients with "alien" limbs gives us powerful reasons to believe that there are brain mechanisms that establish self-reference; it suggests, too, that the claims, made years ago by Henri Claude and by others in our own day, that the limb appears "alien" because its "representation" in the patient's brain has been "destroyed" are inadequate. Why, then, would the space the leg occupies disappear as well? No, what has been destroyed is the mechanism of self-reference—the means by which the leg (and its "place" as well) relates to the body image. The ambiguous nature of an alien leg derives from the conflicting visual evidence that it is attached to parts of the patient's body that do have self-reference (that can feel pain, for example). Self-reference is not a hypothetical idea but a demonstrable part of the structure of consciousness; a partial breakdown in the physiological mechanisms that create it give us the phenomenon of alien limbs.

Of course, the experience of the leg's "alien" nature, like the sense of the teacup's heaviness or lightness, cannot be known without its being expressed linguistically. Knowledge of the experience requires the abstracting, symbolizing categories of language. If this is true, would a patient with an alien limb consider pictures of his leg—another kind of abstract representation—alien as well? When I look at a picture of my hand, my brain "understands" that it is only a picture, a representation, of my hand and not my real hand, partly because it receives no internal sensations from it. Similarly, patients with "alien" limbs recognize them without difficulty as their own *when viewing them in a mirror*! For example, in

1978, Madame W, a sixty-four-year-old woman, came to the hospital paralyzed on her left side.[13] However, she denied that she was paralyzed. Asked to move her left hand, she said, "There!" and moved her right one instead. Told that she had moved her right hand, she looked under the sheets and, failing to find the hand, lost interest in the request. When her left hand was shown to her, she said, "It's not mine, it's yours." "Therefore I have three hands," the examining physician said, and Madame W answered, "Perhaps."

The following day, . . . when shown her left hand, she angrily seized it and tried to give it to the physicians. She considered the hand "foreign."

When she was made to touch her upper [left] arm with her right hand without being allowed to look at what she was doing, she could recognize it as her own. But she no sooner looked at the [left] hand than she declared that it was the doctor's.

This dissociation between the perception of the body by the right hand and the denial by sight inspired us to confront the patient with her image in a mirror. A large mirror was installed on her bed. She recognized herself, finding that she had become thinner. We asked her to use her right hand to find her left: she failed to find it or recognize it, though she could see it both directly and in the mirror. When she was prevented from seeing the hand directly and could only rely on the mirror image, she recognized it immediately. If she was asked to grab her left hand with her right, she had no difficulty carrying out the request. Permitted to look at the left hand directly, however, she immediately released it, saying that it no longer belonged to her. . . . Eventually she was able to become aware of her paralyzed left side in the mirror, a fact that she denied as soon as she once again would [directly] observe her left side.

The mirror image of Madame W's hand is an abstraction, a symbol, but neither the symbol itself nor its significance is fixed. Before she was shown her hand in the mirror, she denied that it belonged to her ("It's yours"); then she recognized it in the mirror; and then again, she said the same hand "no longer belongs to me." This sequence shows, I believe, that no stored image of her hand could be responsible for these very different responses; rather, Madame W recategorized the "memory" of her hand as circumstances changed. Critical to her recategorizations were the immediately preceding circumstances and the form of the self-reference. She might deny that the hand was hers when she looked right at it because she lacked an *immediate* sense of self-reference. But having seen the image of her hand in the mirror, having recognized it (the mirror image being a more abstract—"symbolic"— form of self-reference), and then being shown her "real" hand, she no longer denied that it was hers but instead claimed that it was "no longer" hers (a different form of self-reference, referring to her past). The different forms of self-reference here are different forms of memory; self-reference's complex structure and many different forms are part of the complex structure of memory.

The fragility of memory's structure is such that while some patients treat their paralyzed limbs as "alien," others, with different symptoms, are prepared to accept truly alien limbs as their own, and unable to establish the position of an arm or a leg, they behave as if paralyzed when they are not. One patient, Mr. March, who had lost all positional sense (proprioception) on his left side, could move his left arm only when asked to do so: "One noted a kind of inertia of the left arm to engage in spontaneous movements."[14] March, however, did not have any problems of "neglect." He never offered his right hand, as Babinski's patients did, when asked to raise his left. He always *tried* to show his left hand, even though his injury meant that he did not know where it was. For example, when his left hand was hidden under a drape and a nurse stood behind him, placed her own hand on top of the cloth, and asked him to take his left hand in his right, he took the nurse's hand, looked at it, and caressed it.

March was not troubled that he was holding a woman's hand with a diamond ring and a bracelet. Asked where his own ring was, he said, "It has been taken from me."

And why was he now wearing a bracelet? "It has been put on me."

"But this hand is all white and not as hairy as your own."

"It's like that because it is paralyzed."

When the nurse moved her hand and March was asked why he had moved *his* hand, he said that he couldn't understand why it moved. He was able eventually to figure out that he had been tricked, and he subsequently concluded every time he saw the nurse's hand move that "since it moved it isn't mine." Thereafter, when asked to move his left hand and take it in his right, he moved his left hand under the cloth and unhesitatingly took the nurse's hand, which had not moved, claiming it was his.

Thus March never used his left hand unless told to do so, because on its own his brain did not know where the hand was. But the physician's order to move it helped to locate his arm for him:

[March] never uses his left side without precise orders. . . . He can, however, show his arm or leg. He has a profound disinterest in mobilizing his left side. He readily accepts another's hand as his own, in spite of all the incongruities that one points out to him. He claims that his hand, which has normal mobility, is paralyzed and is only astonished that the nurse's hand, a hand he considers his own, can move.

March's acceptance of the incongruent became particularly evident when, after he acknowledged the nurse's hand on his left side as his, the drape covering his hand was removed: then he accepted both left hands as his own. It was noted that he therefore had ten left fingers. "I don't know," he said; "of course it is odd." "And you have two left hands?" "Well, it makes one wonder." Deeply troubled, he offered various explanations, suggesting that perhaps his left hand had been counted twice. Eventually he learned to pinch his left hand and would comment when pinching the nurse's hand, "This is not my hand, it is someone else's. Why? It is thinner, whiter, and I don't wear a ring."

In the case of March, it was not a matter of reacting to his left side as "alien." It was that he could not locate his arm because he lacked positional sense; he did not know where the arm was. But he did have self-reference; he knew he had an arm, and therefore he was prepared to accept a left arm in the appropriate place as his own. Only when he verified that it was indeed his arm by pinching it could he establish which arm was his. Thus a lack of sense of pain, and hence self-reference, may make limbs "alien;" a lack of sense of position, however, may allow one to believe that an "alien" limb is one's own.

These processes are evident in a child's acquisition of body image and knowledge of space and of objects. For the infant and child, movement, frame of reference, and body image are all interrelated. At the moment of birth, a newborn infant is probably not conscious. Its bodily movements, which are genetically determined reflexes, are the frame of reference within which the baby organizes the stimuli it encounters in its first contacts with the world; as the brain organizes these stimuli, newer stimuli begin to be "understood" in terms of those already organized. The relation between the new and the old brings the first glimmerings of consciousness. Little by little, the infant becomes aware, in however primitive a way, of its surroundings. For sure, this occurs so rapidly that we may have the illusion that the newborn infant is already conscious at birth. But consciousness continually builds on itself; and linguistically, for example, it will be many years before the child will acquire a "full" consciousness that permits it to understand complex ideas (as we shall see in Chapter IV). Initially, in any event, the dynamic of body movement, even when objects and people are not directly touched or explored, is the frame of reference through which a baby's understanding of the world emerges.

For example, at four months of age, the infant's attention begins to be attracted more often to one hand than the other, though the two hands are visually similar and equal. The infant becomes aware of the asymmetry of his hands. An asymmetrical body image begins to emerge in the infant's mind simultaneously with his initial understanding of the nature of objects around him. When the middle of a stick has been hidden from his view, the child will consider the stick a unity if the two ends, though different in color, move uniformly; if the visible ends do not move uniformly, though they are of the same color, the infant will react as if there were two sticks. Infants, the psychologists Kellerman and Spelke have written, do

> not expect surfaces to be connected by virtue of the regularity of their colors and textures, or the goodness of the forms

that can be created by grouping them together. For infants
. . . do not conceive of the world as composed of things that
tend to have simple shapes and uniform substances. . . .
Infants perceive objects by detecting the movements of surfaces and not by analyzing the colors or forms of surfaces.[15]

And a child's first words apparently "depend in part on the
detection of the spatial arrangements and the movements of
surfaces and the groupings of surfaces into objects. Toddlers
readily count and learn new words for connected, bounded
objects." The infant perceives motion, not thanks to "motion
detectors" in the brain, but because the perception of moving
objects is interdependent with the infant's emerging body
image. So, too, the adult's perception of the world depends on
a dynamic body image. It may be—to refine the point further—that the infant's recognition of movement in parts of
its body is the basis for its recognition of objects moving.

The pattern of acquisition of body image and, with it, of
knowledge of objects suggests how central body image is to
our understanding of the world. Notions of space, objects, and
self-reference (which includes emotions, for emotions are part
of the structure of self-reference) depend on body image, and
they cannot be separated. These connections are nicely illus-
trated in the following experiment conducted by the English
psychologist Richard Gregory:

> He constructed a self-luminant outline cube. It is possible
> to invert the cube so that in the dark what appears to be
> its near face is actually the far one. Gregory then asks
> the subject to rotate the cube. . . . Either one observes a
> strange visual distortion of the cube or, alternatively, the
> object remains a cube but one's wrist feels as though it were
> breaking.[16]

In other words, either the space is deformed in reference to oneself or one's body image is deformed! Self-reference is ever-present.

The self-referential character of our sense of space is evident in another kind of "neglect." In a famous case reported in 1978, the Italian neurologists Bisiach and Luzzatti asked two patients who had "left-sided visual neglect" to describe the entire square in front of the Milan Cathedral from memory.[17] When the patients were asked to imagine themselves at the cathedral door, facing away from it, they "remembered" only the buildings on the side of the square to their right. When asked to imagine that they were on the opposite side of the square, facing the cathedral, they again could recall only buildings to the right. Yet curiously, when the patients were asked to describe first one side of the square and then the other, they could do so without difficulty. Like those already discussed, these patients were unable to establish a certain very specific kind of relation to themselves; they had lost not body image but visual left-sided self-reference. They could not visually remember the left side of the square no matter what their vantage point because they could not establish a relation between visual stimuli on the left side and themselves, and therefore there was nothing there for them to visualize. When, however, they were *told* to describe first the left side of the square and then the right side of the square, the question changed the frame of reference to a *verbal* notion of left and right, and the answer was not dependent on their *visual* "left" and "right," and not defined by their visual field; therefore they could establish a self-reference to the entire square.

Of course, one might argue that the memory of the entire square existed in these patients' brains; it was just not always completely available to their consciousness. But why was the memory loss associated with the structure of their visual space? And why, since the patients could recall the entire square from an abstract verbal perspective, were they unable to relate that recollection when given specific instructions to recall the square visually? These patients were not "neglecting" their left visual space, memory of which existed somewhere in their brains. Rather, for them, that space no longer existed visually, although it still had an abstract verbal meaning to which they could relate and hence in verbal terms recreate. Their visual space had been restructured and therefore so were their memories in terms of that space.

If a loss of visual self-reference of this kind deforms a patient's sense of space, the loss of visual space itself alters the body image. This happens with blindness. John Hull, who became blind when he was twenty-four years old, gives a vivid description of the loss of body image in his book *Touching the Rock*:

> I feel as if I am on the borders of conscious life, not just in the literal sense that I am slipping in and out of sleep, but in a deeper and more alarming sense. I feel as if I want to stop thinking, stop experiencing. The lack of a body image makes this worse: the fact that one can't glance down and see the reassuring continuing of one's own consciousness in the outlines of one's own body. . . . There is no extension of awareness into space. . . . I am dissolving. I am no longer concentrated in a particular location, which would be symbolized by the integrity of the body.[18]

When Hull lost his sight he lost a mental image of space. It was not that a stored image of space was erased: the very concept of visual space disappeared, because Hull no longer had a visual frame of reference, a visual body image.

For a blind person, the loss of the visual body image initially destroys the idea of space, destroys visual self-reference, and destroys much knowledge that is inevitably tied into them. Early on in his blindness, Hull reported: "Sometimes I feel that I am being buried in blindness. I am being carried deeper and deeper in. The weight presses me down. Such knowledge as I have is disappearing." His only point of reference became a body that had no extension in space: "I come back to the one thing I know. There is my body, sitting here on the edge of the bed, trembling and sweating. There is the tension in my stomach, the pounding in my temples. I hear my breathing. I feel my heart pounding. I do not know what is out there; I know what is in here."[19]

This body image—created from *internal* sensations—is essential for the blind man's remembering:

> Now and again, back and beyond the occasional visual inspiration, lies something deeper which can be called body-memory. This is not so much memory of what things looked like, but recollections of how things felt. The most vivid of these are usually not of a specific event but of some regular happening. . . .
>
> So it is with the memories of the blind adult. They focus upon what his body has experienced, or underwent. This is quite different from visual memory. . . .

Hull's sense of the past is thus reduced to intimate, immediate sensations of his body in space, moving around a world he once knew in a very different way:

> My memory is like the memory of a snail. My body can recollect the narrow little strip of ground over which I have passed, and it consists of tiny details, so tiny as to be irrelevant from the point of view of the cat and the dog. . . .

When I try to visualize my route [from home to office], what I do is to anticipate the sensations which my body will have at various times (i.e. places) along that route. . . . What lies more than two or three feet away on either side of that trail means nothing to me. It is not part of my experience, except when it comes home to me in traffic noise or birdsong. My place is known to me by the soles of my feet and by the tip of my cane.[20]

Reduced to a body image of touch, hearing, and internal sensation, Hull's recollections, too, were transformed. They were no longer visual. He was now processing his memories as a blind person. For recollection establishes relations to one's present self; a conscious image of the past is created from an integration of a past exeprience and the present reality in terms of the self.

The blind man reduced to the perspective of a snail, the patient who omits the left side of a space when told to imagine himself at a certain point and describe what he sees, and the patient who treats his leg as "alien" are all examples of a profoundly altered subjectivity with consequent transformations of individual knowledge and memory. Blindness reduces the body image to an area in contact with the ground; visual space is lost and, with it, extension and direction. Sound may, to some extent, give the blind important clues about space and extension, but sound lacks the continuity that visual stimuli afford the sighted, and hence its clues are, at best, disconnected. Memories, too, are altered or apparently lost when the blind man adapts to his new frame of reference. So, too, in cases of what is called "visual neglect," the destruction in the brain of the ability to relate the body to a sector of space brings with it an apparent memory loss. Yet it is not that memory has been lost but that visual self-reference has been limited. Much the same happens to patients with alien limbs. All these cases suggest not the loss of any memory traces but rather the subjectivity of memory and its deep connection to consciousness.

In failing to attend to the subjectivity of the conscious self, classical neurology could not give a satisfactory account of the disquieting changes in body image that clinicians elicited from their patients. Some fundamental characteristics of mental function were not part of their models for the brain—for example, the idea of time, central to memory and consciousness, was never mentioned in any of the diagram makers' schemes.

Toward the end of the nineteenth century, a Russian neurologist, Sergei Korsakov (1853–1900), described patients who appeared to lose blocks of memory confined to definite periods of time. By the 1950s, a fortuitous discovery convinced many neurologists and psychologists that the temporal aspects of memories—in particular, the kinds of losses Korsakov had described—were determined by anatomy, much as Wernicke had argued that different kinds of memory were stored in different areas of the brain. Yet they did not trouble themselves with the question of how the brain knew that different memories were in fact from different periods in the individual's life. How does the brain create the notion of time in the first place? This critical question was overlooked. As we shall see, the very concept of time is one important consequence of the mechanisms of subjectivity. It is part of the idea of consciousness.

III

In a World Without Time

In 1887 Sergie Korsakov drew attention to an odd breakdown of memory in certain neurological cases:

> This mental disorder appears at times in the form of a sharply delineated irritable weakness of the mental sphere, at times in the form of confusion with characteristic mistakes in orientation for place, time and situation, at times as an almost pure form of acute amnesia, where the recent memory is most severely involved, while the remote memory is fairly well preserved. . . . In these cases it is most striking, how the same patients who have a good grasp of everything about them and are able to hold an earnest conversation, have suffered so widespread a memory loss that they literally forget everything immediately.[1]

While questions have been raised about the exact nature and extent of such memory defects, the loss of recent memories together with the retention of remote memories is today recognized as a distinct brain disorder, called Korsakov's syndrome. And yet Korsakov's own description of the disorder is oddly insufficient. The distinction between "recent" and "remote" memory is not about memory at all but is a distinction between different ways in which the brain structures knowledge. To view such a neurological disorder as simply a matter of memory loss is to miss its much greater significance. Remote and recent memories are actually different both qualitatively and structurally; our memory of events, people, and situations experienced in the remote past, and their relation to our present self, is quite different from our view of events a week, a month, or even a year ago. Remote memory, or long-term memory as it is known today, and recent, or short-term, memory are different modes of thought; the remote memories are virtual abstractions of everyday existence, and our sense of time, like our sense of change over time, is itself an abstraction. Indeed, we derive our sense of time from the qualitative differences between our remote and recent memories.

Korsakov's syndrome tells us a great deal about how the brain structures knowledge—and memory is a part of this structure. A loss of recent memories is a loss of a specific structure of knowledge, a particular way in which the brain appears to organize stimuli; another way of putting this is to say it is a loss of a particular form of subjectivity, or consciousness. Korsakov's syndrome suggests not that there are different kinds of memories and different storage zones for each kind but rather that there are different kinds of subjectivity and hence different kinds of knowledge, and also that all these forms of subjectivity and knowledge are interrelated. Memory is not an isolated phenomenon but a manifestation of subjective states created by brain activities. And so, too, our notions of time are an integral part of this subjective structure of the brain.

Korsakov's syndrome is the consequence of a profound al-

teration in the structure and nature of the self—or selves—
created by the brain. Oliver Sacks, for example, described a
patient in the 1980s who when asked "How do you feel?"
responded:

"How do I feel," he repeated, and scratched his head. "I
cannot say I feel ill. But I cannot say I feel well. I cannot
say I feel anything at all."
"Are you miserable?"
"Can't say I am."
"Do you enjoy life?"
"I can't say I do. . . ."
"How then *do* you feel about life?"
"I can't say that I feel anything at all."
"You feel alive though?"
"Feel alive? Not really. I haven't felt alive for a very long
time."

Yet Sacks's patient did remember the past; he seemed like a
young man who had never grown up:

his feelings, his innocent wonder, his struggle to make sense
of what he saw, were precisely those of an intelligent young
man in the 1940s faced with the future, with what had not
yet happened, and what was scarcely imaginable. . . . His
cut-off around 1945 is genuine. . . . What I showed him,
and told, produced the authentic amazement which it would
have done in an intelligent young man of the pre-Sputnik
era.[2]

Dramatic new light appeared to be shed on some aspects of
this disorder when Brenda Milner and W. B. Scoville reported
in 1957 that following surgical removal of an area of the brain

called the hippocampus, a patient, H.M., lost recent memories but retained long-term ones.[3] The patient's problem was not exactly like that of the Korsakov patients, for he could remember an experience for as long as fifteen minutes, and Korsakov patients tend to have very little, if any, retention of immediately past events. Nonetheless, this discovery led to a number of suggestions about how the hippocampus was crucial in the brain's converting short-term memories to long-term memories. By the 1970s, however, these ideas were abandoned and replaced with other models of long-term memory. It was argued, for example, that the meanings of words and other verbal symbols are stored separately from memories of personal experiences, and that verbal memories enter long-term storage directly, bypassing the short-term memory mechanisms.[4] Oddly, nobody considered that these different kinds of memory might be interrelated and that the neurological "evidence" that they were independent was based on a presumption that when the patient named an object, the name meant to him what it meant to the examiner. The profound changes in the patient's subjective world were overlooked, especially the deepest clue of all: the patients had lost the sense of time. What did it mean to a patient to "recall" an event from his distant past when he had little or no idea about the present? Even the apparently objective naming of objects was unreliable. What, for example, does a "clock" mean to a patient who now has no real sense of time? Or a "teacup," which might normally suggest morning tea or a late-afternoon drink with friends? Not only do objects have temporal associations, but "what they are" to a person cannot be separated from a person's notion of time.

What might be a more accurate assessment of the importance of the hippocampus in determining our notions of self? The hippocampus is closely linked anatomically to parts of the brain that regulate the body's internal mechanisms such as heartbeat, digestion, and respiration; one might then quite plausibly argue that injury to the hippocampus, in destroying the relation between external and internal stimuli, destroys the ability to create a "memory" that will have a meaningful relation to self. But long-term memories just as much as short-term ones (even verbal ones) require a sense of self; they, too, are created in reference to the self whose memories they are. In what ways is the "self" with long-term memories different from (or similar to) the "self" of short-term memories? Perhaps more important, can we really describe these "selves" as independent? Surely they must depend on each other. The "self" linked to time past is an abstraction of the self-referential "I" that establishes immediate relations to its surroundings.

In the immediate self-centered universe, all objects and actions are understood in terms of the individual "I"; in a more abstract world, created by the brain's generalization of the immediate stimuli, the self is able to perceive and understand that people and actions and objects may refer to each other as well; this is a world of I, You, and the Other. The ability to make these distinctions in the immediate world depends on a notion of "self" that is similar to the "self" structured in terms of its past experience of events, people, and places. On the other hand, if I become unable to maintain an immediate relation to the world for more than a few seconds or minutes, my ability to create new abstractions is bound to be severely limited or even nonexistent, though the kinds of abstraction I learned to make before my injury may remain. Then it will appear that I have no short-term memory but retain long-term memory. But are those long-term "memories" really memories in the conventional sense of the word? They cannot bear any relation to the immediate; they will be out of joint.

Though I may seem to be recalling the past, from my point of view it is not really the past at all, for the usual idea of a past is always in relation to a sense of the present, which I lack. An examining physician may think of my recollections as my remembering the "past," as my "long-term memory," but this description fails to capture the subjective nature of such mental acts. In fact, they are probably unlike anything a normal person could possibly know.

When patients with Korsakov's syndrome say something like "I haven't felt alive for a very long time," they are describing a sense of aliveness largely unconnected to the immediate present. And most curiously, they have to some extent lost a sense of their own body. For what else is "not feeling alive" than that? This loss of body image and, with it, of a sense of self existing in the present has somehow occurred because of damage to the hippocampus (or interconnected areas). And it is related, too, to the odd condition of retaining "remote" or "long-term memory" in the absence of "short-term memory."

In one of the earliest reported cases of loss of short-term memory, the French neurologists H. Mabille and A. Pitres in 1913 described a patient, Henri Baud, who was forty-eight years old and had been in a hospital in La Rochelle for thirteen years. He was unable to remember anything that had happened to him after his thirtieth year.[5] In his daily life, Baud was like "a kind of automaton, calm and indifferent to what was going on around him. He had no recollection of what he saw, of what he did, or of people around him." He had no sense of continuity in the present, no goals, no long-range understanding of how one action was related to another, but, at best, only a fleeting sense of his surroundings and a fleeting notion of self. He performed all acts by imitation, as if his only sense of self was gained by imitating another. And he showed not the slightest concern that he could not understand what he was doing. Imitation may have been an attempt to understand, but it failed because he had no sense of a continuous self that could connect and interrelate the imitated acts, that could make him aware not only of himself but that there was anything to understand. In the mornings he dressed himself only when others did likewise, and in the course of the day he did various jobs in the garden in imitation of others performing gardening tests. "Alone, he was incapable of using any tool or carrying out any task. And unless he was accompanied, he was unable to go from one place to another."

The virtual lack of any sense of self was evident, too, in his inability to understand his relation to others:

> In his personal relations he showed an extraordinary lack of awareness. He did not recognize his comrades, he failed to acknowledge any favor done him, and he showed no preference for one person or another. He had no friends and no enemies; everyone was a stranger. . . . He rarely spoke to anyone spontaneously, but if he was addressed, he would look fixedly at the person and almost always said, "I think that I know you . . . I have seen you before, but I don't know where . . . probably in Paris." He said this to people he was meeting for the first time as well as to those he saw from day to day.

> Baud ate when others ate, indifferent to the quality of the food or whether or not he had already eaten. He had no recollection of eating. "We made him taste some aloes, which he found very bitter," Mabille and Pitres wrote. "Twenty seconds later we asked him if what we had given him was good to eat. He answered that he hadn't had anything to eat and that he was hungry."

And yet for brief moments he occasionally had a sense that he understood, that he knew what he was doing. But these were isolated incidents and had no relation to anything going on around him. When, for example, he did have an opinion and others failed to agree with him, he became angry and insistent, then violent. "Though of a mild disposition, he could not tolerate being contradicted. . . . He became violent, throwing himself upon and trying to strangle whomever failed to agree with him. But once the argument had ended, he showed not the slightest hint of bitterness, behaving as if nothing had happened." His anger expressed a momentary sense of self, a feeling of understanding. But it was too isolated, and then he became violent in his insistence that people grasp his isolation; thereafter his anger dissipated into his unremembered past.

When Henri Baud was asked something about his past, and only when he was asked, he appeared to recall it. But one can see that these were habitual responses; even when they seemed quite specific, they were part of a pattern. When asked "Do you like women?" he could answer, "Very much." When further asked "Do you have any mistresses?" he appeared to give a specific answer: "Yes. At the moment, I have a woman in the rue Cambacérès, whose lover I am. She is well taken care of, and I go there every Saturday night." Asked "When did you last see her?" he responded, "Last Saturday," though he had not left the hospital for thirteen years. These were habitual acts and habitual ways of thought. They were not answers about remembered, specific events. They appeared to be specific, and yet they described only what had once been a general pattern of behavior.

When we recall the past we think in a more general or abstract mode than when we recall recent events. Distant experiences become specific—refer to a specific event in our past—when we can relate them to our present world. When Baud said he had seen his mistress "last Saturday," he had no idea of the actual day of the week, month, or year; he could not have meant a specific Saturday, because he did not understand how "last Saturday" was related to his present, any more than he could understand the idea of "two Saturdays ago," other than as a general formula in a pattern. He could make a certain kind of sense of the physicians' questions and respond to them, because he did sustain brief periods of experience (twenty-odd seconds) in his head. But since he could not do this for longer spans of time (days, weeks), his responses could not possibly have any general relation to his present experience. His apparently specific "recollections" were only indications of the larger abstract nature of his sense of the past, an abstract awareness that is all but impossible—for any of us who have not suffered his injury—to characterize. We cannot imagine what "last Saturday" could have meant to Baud. Even his memory of the town of La Rochelle, where he was hospitalized, was part of a general way of "thinking" about the past that we must acknowledge is a mystery to us. The words La Rochelle recalled to him a night in a brothel; this summed up all he knew of La Rochelle:

"Do you know La Rochelle?"
"Yes, I went there some time ago."
"Why?"
"To wander about."
"Where did you stay?"
"Rue des Voiliers."
"You know someone there?"
"No. I was given the address and told it was a good place to find pretty women. . . . So I went there, found a woman, and slept with her. Then I returned to Paris."

"Did you see anything interesting in La Rochelle?"
"Absolutely nothing."
"Did you see the sea?"
"Never. But I'd like very much to."
"Did you ever go back to La Rochelle?"
"Never."

How *do* we measure the passage of time? Past time becomes truly specific only in relation to the immediate present; and time in the immediate sense is measured by our physical relation to our surroundings—the movements of our body. People who can see, the blind John Hull said, "measure time by seeing movement." But blind people are denied this perception of time as a visual relation between the individual and his surroundings; being reduced to the position of his or her own body, the blind person can judge time only by how long the body has been in motion. The blind, having no sense of the distance of physical goals, become aware of events after, not as, they happen; the world of the immediate is lost, and the world of the future is difficult to judge. Dependence on bodily movements becomes monotonous, and the blind have the feeling that time hardly passes. They experience, as Hull says, "time-inflation."[6] Of course, the blind still have a sense of the present; they can establish relations between events of yesterday and today, though they may feel that this is an enormous span of time. But when, as in Baud's case, the present is virtually lost, "time-inflation" becomes infinite and recollections become odd abstractions, devoid of temporal meaning.

In sharp contrast to the patients I have discussed so far are individuals whose "self-centered" view of the world suggests an inability to understand any point of view other than their own. "I" as opposed to "you" does not exist for them; an "object" can be perceived to exist in relation to the "I" but not in relation to another object. In the conventional literature, these patients are said to have short-term but no long-term memory. But once again, these terms overlook the deeper psychological and physiological differences.

Adhémar Gelb and Kurt Goldstein, for example, in 1933 described a patient who "no longer really knows anyone but herself; things only have value in terms of herself. . . . This self-centered attitude . . . is not the consequence of moral change but a reflection of changes in a more general attitude. . . . It is particularly evident in her use of language."[7] When the patient was unable to list some women's first names and Gelb and Goldstein insisted, she finally produced four names, which she identified as those of her four sisters. She could not at first give a general list of animals, and when she ultimately did name a few, she explained that they were the names one came upon when walking through the zoo—and she presented them in the very order in which she had encountered them during her walks in the zoological park. She could not organize a collection of skeins of wool by color, though she could organize them in a pattern similar to that on one of her dresses or scarves. When pressed to group the skeins by color, she became agitated and said, "This is completely false. It doesn't work." Figurative or abstract words she would understand only literally. (*Backfisch*, the German word for "adolescent," which literally means "fish for frying," she understood as "one fries fish.") She did not understand proverbs or comparisons. "The patient could name all the ordinary objects without difficulty," Goldstein noted, "but this usage was not accompanied by any conceptual attitude concerning the objects. One had the impression that these words had a different sense than for a normal person."[8]

In general, Gelb and Goldstein's patient failed to understand nouns in any abstract sense, though she could see them in concrete situations in which she played an active role. Simple descriptions of events that did not directly concern her were beyond her comprehension, while complicated descriptions of matters that affected her directly were readily understood.

Most strikingly, Gelb and Goldstein's patient never spoke spontaneously, only reacting to others' questions and orders. She responded to the immediate; there was no "long-term" point of view.

The patient's only problem is to integrate and arrange everything in her present activity. . . . She does not "understand," "seize," "remark," or "retain" what is asked of her. . . . Outside of this limited sphere there are no issues for the patient, and she becomes totally lost. . . .

Heinrich von Kleist noted . . . that when one is not sure about an issue, one must not begin by thought and reflection on the theme; it is better to *talk* calmly about it. . . . The French say, The appetite comes with eating. One might parody this by saying, Thought comes when one speaks. . . . This attitude, true of most people, should be contrasted with our patient, who also begins by "talking" without knowing where she is going, but who never gets beyond the level of the . . . "immediate."[9]

When we say in normal experience that thought comes while one speaks, we mean that thought thus moves from an immediate to a more abstract mode; thought builds on itself; the immediate and the abstract become connected—indeed, one cannot exist without the other. If we knew only the immediate world of our senses, we could never describe it as such, any more than we could describe our thoughts as being "abstract" or general if that was the only kind of intellection we experienced.

In a sense, we can never know and scarcely can imagine what a Korsakov patient is "thinking" or what a patient like Gelb and Goldstein's is "thinking." We cannot truly grasp his or her subjective world. Since we find his way of talking about the world odd, we try to describe it in terms of *our* understanding of the world. And therefore we say that he has only an "immediate" relation to his surroundings, or only an "abstract" relation. But in reality the patient, lacking one, has neither, just as he cannot have one kind of memory without the other. From the point of view of the patient, his or her "memories" are not memories; the very nature of memory has drastically changed.

To make a distinction between long- and short-term memory or between abstract and immediate knowledge may be useful clinically, but in making it we fall into the same trap as the diagram makers did. We must try to understand that our relation to the world is not sometimes abstract and sometimes immediate but, rather, *always both*. Both our ability to remember things from the distant past and the procedures we use for our "short-term" memory have been acquired and refined over time. Certain kinds of brain damage give clinicians the illusion that they can isolate specific brain functions and see them at work. But the peculiarity of those functions when operating separately is a warning that they are not what they appear to be. Mabille and Pitres presumed, as many neurologists have since, that when Baud said he saw his mistress "last Saturday," he was referring to a specific Saturday from before his illness. Yet from Baud's point of view, this was impossible; he had no sense of time, and therefore "last Saturday" could not have a specific meaning. We must be more careful in trying to decide what a patient means when he or she responds to clinical inquiries. In a sense, the responses cannot be classified in the usual ways. Indeed, the remarkable ease of our normal human ability to slide back and forth from the past to the present, from a generalizing thought to a specific experience, suggests not that in doing so we are moving from one world to the other, one mode of thought to another, but that there is a deep connection between these modes and memories that the clinicians are failing to grasp. Memory is rooted in our sense of time, and our sense of time is a set of relations of which memory is a part. Memory and time are inseparable and are created anew when we try to imagine events of yesterday, a week ago, or forty years ago. They are part of the very structure of conscious knowledge.

It is not, then, that images are stored somewhere in the brain, as Wernicke suggested and as many studies in artificial intelligence still assume. There is no place in the brain storing a fixed image of Mary, John, or Jane, and in fact, we never think of or remember people in fixed images. It has been argued that if memory images are not fixed, at least the categories of knowledge, our ways of generalizing, must be, that there must be innate programs in the brain. But if this were true, then specific brain damage would reveal the specific functions, the programs—and indeed, many scientists and neurologists believe this is exactly what they do reveal. Yet Baud's "last Saturday" reveals no specific category of knowledge; we have no idea exactly what Baud meant by these two words. What they reveal is a more global form of brain activity from which meaning emerges, and in his case the activity—the interactions of stimuli in terms of the body-image frame of reference—had been severely impaired.

The possible physiological basis of some of these brain processes was suggested by Gerald Edelman in 1978.[10] Edelman challenged the idea that the brain could have innate programs that create fixed categories of knowledge. He argued that since genes cannot determine the exact connections of nerve cells, it would be impossible to program a brain, just as it would be impossible to program a computer in which the wiring was not exactly predetermined. No two organisms and hence no two brains can ever be exactly alike, not even those of identical twins.

But if no two brains are alike, what are the common principles underlying their functioning? In Edelman's view, the brain functions as a system based on selection. In 1978 he proposed that nerve cells tend to form into strongly interconnected groups called neuronal groups. Because each group of neurons has its own pattern of internal connections (the exact interconnections of nerve cells cannot be genetically determined), it will respond differently to various stimuli, even identical stimuli, and it may respond to many different stimuli. After repeated excitation by similar stimuli, its response will be reinforced: some of the groups will come to respond better to certain stimuli on later occasions and some that had initially responded weakly will not respond at all. Thus environmental stimuli select neuronal groups.

Neuronal groups are organized into sheets of brain tissue that neuroscientists call maps, and the neuronal groups within a given map tend to respond to similar kinds of stimulus. The neuronal groups in one map may respond to the color of a visual stimulus, say, while those in another map may respond to the direction of its movement. The various maps are interconnected by networks of nerves, and in the presence of a particular stimulus, the responses of the different maps will be coordinated by an exchange of signals among them and a coherent response will emerge. This coherent response Edelman misleadingly calls a "perceptual categorization" of the stimulus. What makes it a categorization (and Edelman fails to recognize this) is its relation to other coherent responses. Categories are relations.* Hence it is not the individual coherent response that is important but the relation of different coherent responses to each other.

How categorization of a stimulus is achieved might be best understood by analogy. Imagine, for example, a group of musicians, let us say a string quartet. As each member of the quartet plays his individual instrument, he both sends to and receives from his fellow musicians "signals" about the sound, volume, rhythm, accent, and tone quality of the music. Each player is carrying on an individual dialogue with the other players, together creating a sound at any given moment. There is no conductor, no central command. So, too, in the brain, local interactions among the brain's maps, their "speaking" back and forth to each other by an exchange of signals, creates a coherent response to a stimulus. The response to the stimulus is not predetermined; local interactions among different parts of the brain give the response its coherence. Just as the shape and overall sound of the quartet's performance is created by the various sounds from moment to moment, so, too, categorizations emerge from the brain's relating one coherent response to another and another.

Indeed, patterns often emerge over time without any predetermined goals. William Clancey, an expert in artificial intelligence, proposed a traffic jam as

a good example . . . because it is clearly not deliberately organized. A bottleneck may form where roads converge or narrow. The individual cars are not following a plan for "how to participate in a traffic back-up" or even "how to create today's traffic back-up." The organization that observers see in the lines of cars was not predescribed, but is

*See page 98.

a structure that emerges through the interaction of many parts. There is no scheduler deciding what car gets to move next. Observers will see patterns in the emergent behavior over time (e.g., as a bottleneck becomes released just beyond the scene of an accident, even hours after the area has been cleared away). But there is no "pattern"—some*thing*—that is being "followed" (interpreted) by the participants.[11]

Recent neurophysiological evidence appears to confirm that the brain creates coherent patterns of responses to stimuli. In two separate laboratories in Germany it was found that groups of nerve cells in the cat tend to oscillate together at a particular frequency in response to a visual stimulus. The different oscillatory patterns are a consequence of the varying internal connectivity from group to group. However, in the presence of a stimulus, groups even in different parts of the brain oscillate coherently at the same frequency.[12] How the brain relates these coherent patterns of response from moment to moment remains unknown.

The coherent responses are not conscious, for consciousness arises from the further dynamic interrelations of the past, the present, and the body image. This central interrelation is the factor that physiological and scientific theories have overlooked. Recognition and understanding are dynamic, emerging in an ongoing flow of images that depends on dynamic relations. The object or person I am aware of, that I recognize at any given moment, has a dynamic relation to the same object or person an instant before. A murder clue suddenly makes sense; its relation to the past takes on a new significance. The change in its significance is not in the direct perception of the clue at the given moment but in its relation to what went before.

So, too, consciousness in general is dynamic. Hence Head's

claim that recognition of body posture is "already charged with its relation to something that has gone before." For at the very moment the brain is establishing coherent responses, new stimuli are arriving that will alter them; these dynamic changes will continue as long as we are conscious. It is the very process of change that rises to consciousness, that *is* consciousness; awareness is change, not the direct perception of stimuli. Conscious images are dynamic relations among a flow of constantly evolving coherent responses, at once different and yet derived from previous responses that are part of an individual's past.

What makes consciousness is the subjective nature of the responses. And the neurological evidence has suggested that subjectivity derives from the relationship between the dynamic body image (itself a series of coherent responses) and \
the dynamic progression of coherent responses to new stimuli: these self-referential mechanisms are the basis of feeling conscious and of an individual's knowledge. When brain damage destroys specific aspects of self-reference, it alters the structure of consciousness, hence knowledge as well. Baud's injury meant that he could sustain a sense of body image for only about twenty seconds, too brief a span for him to establish a sense of time. His self-consciousness, his self-awareness, was thus deeply altered. His "last Saturday" was, at best, abstract; for him, "last Saturday" floated in a timeless world not relating to any specific day past or present.

What has apparently been damaged in such cases is either the hippocampus or associated structures in an area of the brain known as the limbic system, first described and named by Paul Broca in 1878. The limbic system is a kind of way station anatomically linked to much of the brain. It is a group of interconnected structures that appears to form a border deep inside the brain (the Latin *limbe* means "border").

In 1937 James Papez of Cornell University suggested that the limbic system and a small structure at the base of the brain, the hypothalamus, have an important function in emotional behavior and in the maintenance of temperature, heartbeat, respiration, and other bodily processes. Many of the processes that manifest themselves in "emotional" states—increased heartbeat, sweating, rapid breathing—are under the control of the hypothalamus. Papez argued that the higher brain centers communicate with the hypothalamus through the complicated circuitry of the limbic system, which appeared to be the "center" for emotions.[13]

At about the same time, Heinrich Klüver and Paul Bucy at the University of Chicago performed an experiment in which they destroyed different parts of the limbic system in monkeys.[14] The animals became tame, put any object they could lay their hands on into their mouths, were hypersensitive to all stimuli, were sexually overactive, and showed a complete lack of fear or anger. In humans, damage to the limbic system causes profound changes in emotional reactions and memory. In fact, it has been found that whenever a person is remembering, there is activity in the limbic system.[15] It may be that the limbic system is essential for establishing the correlations between body image and external stimuli that are the basis of consciousness.

A conscious image, then, whether recognition or recollection, is the consequence of complex neurophysiological interactions; in it the person's past and present experiences are integrated, and the subjective, self-referential quality is of its very essence. The constantly evolving generalizations that emerge are a fundamental characteristic of human psychology. What we call experience, or history, is this endless progressive structuring of events. We rewrite history, we revise our notions of our experiences, by restructuring our thought about people and events in our past. We may, at one point in time, think of Arthur and Jane as "the most wonderful couple" we have ever known; and we may, later, think we have never met "two more awful people." Historians constantly rewrite history, reinterpreting (reorganizing) the records of the past. So, too, when the brain's coherent responses become part of a memory, they are organized anew as part of the structure of consciousness. What makes them memories is that they become part of that structure and thus form part of the sense of self; my sense of self derives from a certainty that my experiences refer back to *me*, the individual who is having them. Hence the sense of the past, of history, of memory, is in part the creation of the self.

These higher forms of consciousness certainly require language, but having language does not guarantee that conscious awareness will not be eroded by neurological disease. Patients' verbal reports often give evidence of altered states of consciousness of which the patients are unaware: in other words, the neurological alteration of linguistic function shows an altered consciousness. It is all the stranger that neurologists and neuroscientists have for so long studied linguistic function independently of the structure of consciousness. Language, after all, arises from the same kinds of neurophysiological process as nonlinguistic forms of consciousness. As we shall see, with the evolutionary development of brain areas that could create a "consciousness of consciousness," language emerged in ways strikingly parallel to the brain's ability to create a dynamic self-referential system. Relations among sets of stimuli from moment to moment are consciousness; language, too, is made up of relations, whose abstract nature is the ultimate form of consciousness.

IV

Language: Prime Cuts

At the end of the nineteenth century, the French neurologist Jean-Martin Charcot (1825–1893) captured the flavor of much orthodox neurological thought in a charming description of the mechanisms of speech and writing. His description, indeed, bears an uncanny resemblance to many discussions of brain function in our own day, and it is worth reproducing his diagram and accompanying explanation in full (see facing page).[1]

Charcot believed that a word was

> a complex entity made of at least four fundamental elements: the auditory memory image, the visual memory image, and two motor images, one for speaking (articulation) and one for writing. . . . Thus when an idea presents itself, one can call upon either the auditory image or the visual image of the word that characterizes the idea. . . . When one fails to understand written words, we say one has verbal blindness or visual verbal amnesia, and when one cannot recognize the sounds of spoken words, we call the affliction

Professor Charcot's Diagram of Articulate and Written Language

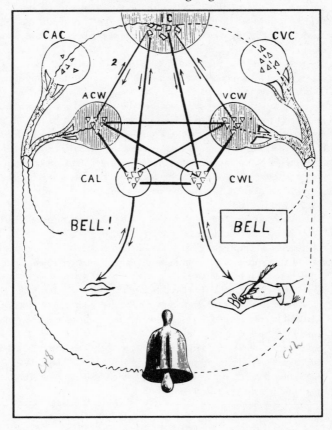

IC, Ideational Center

CAC, Common Auditive Center	CVC, Common Visual Center
ACW, Auditive Center of Words	VCW, Visual Center of Words
CAL, Center of Articulate Language	CWL, Center of Written Language

A bell is supposed to ring near a child; the sound makes an impression upon the peripheral expansion of the acoustic nerve and is conveyed by the nerve itself to a sensitive cell in the cerebral cortex, in that region which constitutes the *common auditive center* (CAC), where it forms a deposit and effects some slight permanent change.

The word "bell" is pronounced before the child, and this sound is also conveyed by the acoustic nerve to the *auditive center of words* (ACW), the center specially organized for the intelligent perception of articulate speech.

The impressions thus produced are registered in the child's *ideational center* (IC), and he associates the word "bell" with the recollection of the sound previously heard.

In order to designate the bell to others by the word thus learnt and retained, and to give outward expression to this "sound image," it is necessary to be able to pronounce it, and the education of a new center is necessary; the auditive center of words having supplied the child with an internal image of the sound required, he transfers it to the *center of articulate language* (CAL), which enables him to regulate and coordinate the movements of the organ for the articulation of words, and the child speaks the word "bell."

A similar process is supposed to take place in reference to the visual and graphic aspect of language.

A bell is placed before the child's eyes, an impression is made upon the retina and transmitted by the optic nerve to the *common visual center* (CVC), where it forms a deposit.

The written word "bell" is placed before the child, and by means of the optic nerve, the written sign is conveyed to the *visual center of words* (VCW), and the image thus produced is registered in the *ideational center* (IC), as in the case of the auditive bell image.

In order to enable the child to write the word "bell," the internal image of which has been supplied to him by his *visual center of words* (VCW), another center is called into action, the *center of written language* (CWL), and the child is able to write the word "bell."

---

verbal deafness or auditory verbal amnesia. Similarly, according to the same principles, we can say that one has motor verbal amnesia when the motor images of words are lost. . . . And it should not be forgotten that there are a variety of individual mechanisms for recalling words; the most common is the use of the auditory memory image to translate the idea into its corresponding sign; others use the visual memory image; and still others one of the motor memory images.

There are also those who use mixed forms of memory images.[2]

Charcot did not, of course, think that visual and auditory memory was limited to words. He knew one could lose *all* visual memories, as happened to one patient, Monsieur A, who before his illness had an unusual ability for visual recollection.[3] He could recall people in such detail that it seemed to him that he was bodying them forth as they actually were. He could recall details of handwritten letters—the page on which a given word had been written, the places where words had been crossed out. If he read a book two or three times, he could visualize any page in it and "read" it aloud from memory. And he could reproduce all the details of a dramatic performance he had attended, including the gestures of the actors.

"Monsieur A had traveled widely," Charcot noted. "He liked to draw sites and perspectives with which he had been particularly impressed. He drew very well. He could recall entire panoramas in great detail."

His recollections were never of isolated details but of entire scenes, and the scenes may have had for him an abstract, symbolic quality. Indeed, it was this complex, symbolic quality of Monsieur A's visual images that was extraordinary. When trying to recall a conversation, a phrase, or a word, he first recalled where the conversation had taken place, the appearance of the speaker, and his or her gestures; similarly, he had first to visualize an entire page of a book (and its number) in order to recall a particular passage on it. He could establish these complex relations visually although not aurally; music, for example, meant nothing to him. His visual images had, one might say, the complex structure of words. And it was the complexity of this structure that was his memory.

One day things changed. Monsieur A became disoriented,

lost his memory for shapes and colors, and became dependent on "other forms of memory." Everything appeared unfamiliar. He walked about the streets of his hometown astonished by buildings and monuments that were once familiar to him. Where formerly he had been able to make accurate drawings from memory, he now produced little more than crude and often unrecognizable representations. He said that he *knew* the structure of a building or monument he was attempting to draw (an "arcade," a "semicircle") but he could not *see* it "in reality." He even had difficulty drawing a tree and represented it with unformed scribblings. Asked to trace a picture of a tree, he said, "I don't know how it is done."

He could not imagine his wife and children. At first he failed to recognize them, as he had the streets of his hometown, and then he said they seemed to have changed. Nor could he recognize himself in a mirror: walking in a public gallery, he suddenly noticed that his passage was blocked, stepped aside, and excused himself. He was looking at his own image in a mirror.

We can see now—although this was not how Charcot put it—that Monsieur A had lost much of his visual self-reference; he could still actually see, but what he saw had become almost meaningless—alien and unrecognizable. The nature of his essential selfhood, his subjectivity, his relation to his surroundings, had changed. It is important to note that when visual experience becomes so constrained, visual memories seem inevitably to disappear; visual recognition and recollection become virtually impossible. Monsieur A had no idea how what he was seeing related to himself or his past— whether it was city streets, or his own image in a mirror, or his wife. This loss of visual memories has often been noted by sighted people who become blind. When the brain is unable normally to organize visual stimuli in terms of the individual self-reference, as is the case with a blind person, it cannot

organize visual "memories" either; an essential element in
the creation of memories has been destroyed. It is not that
there were fixed images stored in his unconscious to which
Monsieur A's brain lost access; rather, his entire process of
memorial construction and reconstruction had broken down.
Indeed, a deep clue to the breakdown of the self-referential
mechanisms is that Monsieur A also had lost, to some extent,
the sense of pleasure and pain, and we have seen how this was
true in the other cases previously discussed. "One of the
remarkable consequences of the loss of this mental faculty,"
Monsieur A noted, "is the change in my character and my
impressionability. I am less susceptible to sorrow or psychological pain."

Nonetheless, Monsieur A could still speak, and spoken
words inevitably have self-reference; it is part of their structure. Thus he could dream in words, not images. And his
memories were of what he had *heard*; no visual images came
to mind:

> If you asked me to imagine the spires of Notre Dame, a
> sheep grazing, or a ship in distress on the high seas, I would
> have to tell you that although I know perfectly well how to
> distinguish these very different things and I know what they
> are about, visually they have no meaning for me. . . . Today
> I can remember things only if I can say them to myself,
> while in the past I had only to photograph them with my
> sight.

So he had not lost his memory; memories that were once
visual took "other forms," in "violent" contrast to the world
as he had once known it: "My wife has black hair. I can no
more imagine that color than I can imagine what she looks
like."

So Monsieur A could go on using words, but he could not

imagine for himself what they referred to visually. But of course this possibility is what words are all about. We may be able to discuss a physicist's ten-dimensional universe and yet be unable to visualize it. We don't have to see a table—either in real life or in our mind's eye—in order to understand the word "table," and when we read the word, most of us can understand it without having to visualize it. Words transcend the sensory domains to which they refer. And yet they are a consequence of the very same brain processes that make us conscious of visual, tactile, auditory, and olfactory stimuli in the first place; they are a further elaboration of these processes; they are the result of interactions of much greater complexity. A grasp of language, which of course requires verbal memory, is considerably more complex than Charcot and other neurologists suggested, and his claim that there are specific auditory, visual, and tactile "memory images" of individual words belies the very nature of language. Charcot's own study of Monsieur A illustrates this: for Monsieur A, language—thinking with words—was more abstract than any of these specific sensory categories. He knew Notre Dame, a sheep grazing, or a ship in distress *verbally*, as ideas, that transcended the notions of seeing, hearing, smelling, or touching.

Monsieur A had been, in some sense, very lucky to retain his linguistic capabilities. For words created a continuity for him that would not have been possible with visual images alone. As Henry Head wrote in 1926:

Words and other symbols knit together and give permanence to non-verbal processes of thought, which would otherwise be fleeting. This is particularly evident in the case of visual images. Should an aphasic possess this kind of memory in a strongly developed form, images may still arise spontaneously and play a considerable part in his mental processes. But he cannot evoke them at will or to command; nor can he unite them to a coherent logical sequence without the help of verbal symbols. They are episodic, fleeting and transient; they arise and perish without leaving behind them any permanent or certain addition to thought. Without names we cannot record their relation in time or space, nor their essential likeness or difference.[4]

When one of Head's patients was

asked to describe how he would walk from the hospital to the War Office, he said he could see the big stores, Westminster Abbey and other buildings he would meet on his way. Each appeared as an isolated event; he could not connect them together and pass with ease from one to the other, in consequence of his want of names. He explained that it was "all in bits," and that he had to "jump from one thing to the other" because he "had no names." For, normally, as each image arises it is fixed by its name or some other appropriate formula, and the final conclusion is recorded as a conceptual statement. Images are less easily manipulated than words; they appear and disappear without being strictly connected in logical sequence. Without some verbal form of symbolic substitution it is impossible to express their essential likeness and difference or their significant relations in time and space.

However vivid and detailed these visual images may be, they are elusive and fleeting; the patient complains, "They seem to go faint and I can't get them when I want to." Once aroused, they recur insistently in no obvious connection with the train of thought, or they disappear before the task is completed. One image not infrequently ousts its predecessor, instead of being added to it.[5]

Language connects, interrelates, and abstracts images; it distances us from the immediate, creating a past, a present, and a future; it enriches our awareness of the myriad ways in which our experience of the world can be organized; and it can create a world of its own.

But what are these "names" and "words" that were lost to Head's patients? And exactly how do they create interconnections and a sense of time? John Hull has noted that for the blind, to know someone is to know his or her name: "Sighted people get to know each other by recognizing each other's appearance. . . . The name of the person is one additional item of information, but the appearance is the central core around which everything gathers. For me, knowing someone hangs upon knowing the name. It is the same with streets."[6] When neurological disorder or trauma causes the loss of the ability to name, the loss may be restricted to very specific items. In 1925, for example, Gelb and Goldstein reported the case of a patient who was unable to name the color of an object. He had no response to the words "red," "green," or "blue" and chose an object at random when asked to pick the red one. Told to sort skeins of wool by color, he tended to separate them into pairs and leave them in their original order. On different occasions he created different arrangements. "One might have thought that, for one reason or another, he was changing the rules that he used for ordering the colors. . . . In fact, he was not using any principle of classification, for he was unable to decide what properties he should use for the task of sorting. His behavior was determined by the convenience of the moment."[7]

Nonetheless, the patient had no difficulty choosing and matching items of identical color from a myriad of differently colored ones. He pedantically rejected as inappropriate matches that were not exact, and yet, having matched two items of the same color, he could not name the color, though he could discuss colors when using concrete examples, such as "cherry red" or "grass color" or "like an orange." "When one has only an *immediate and practical* relation with the world of colors," Goldstein noted, "and when one has lost *abstract relations*, words such as red, blue, green, etc., lose their 'representative' meanings. . . . [They are no longer] symbols for the concept of color."

This "concrete" use of language, tied only to the immediate facts, was part of the patient's general behavior: "Language only serves a 'representative' function when it is part of a more general behavioral pattern . . . [that is] categorical."[8] He sorted colors without a general categorical sense, but only in accordance with the dictates of the moment; and he did this in a fussy, pedantic, wholly absorbed way. Of course, a perfectly normal person may plunge into an activity with a meticulousness that seems little different from this patient's. We have all experienced moments of concentrated activity of this kind. "The more we act in an immediate fashion, . . . the less the 'distance' between us and the objects, the more exacting and precise our actions and the more . . . 'automatic' and unconscious."

But the resemblance between normal and abnormal here is superficial, for in retrospect we can relate our actions to a larger whole, while this patient's actions remained isolated and unrelated. We, though deeply lost in a particular activity, will reconsider what we are doing if sudden changes force us to, while this patient was little bothered by new "facts," and when they did attract his attention, he became upset and disoriented. In normal experience, new facts may "shake us up" and we may become "disturbed," but we are not disoriented: "our relation to the immediate is broken. This 'disturbance,' this 'awareness' or 'distance,' is not only characteristic of human beings, but is what distinguishes us from the patho-logical. In the latter cases, sudden 'awareness' does not result in 'knowing,' but rather in a sense of total confusion and anxiety, and an inability to react."[9]

The process of naming, then, is like the process that leads to knowledge; it implies understanding of the object named. Names establish relationships between us and other people (friends, cousins, fellow citizens) or between us and events or objects. Goldstein stresses the categorical nature of names, and he notes that with certain types of brain damage, this function may be clinically lost:

> Analysis of patients with difficulty in finding words has revealed that there is an essential difference as to the attitude of the individual—corresponding to the differentiation we make. When the patient truly "names" an object, he has the experience of a word which "means" this object, consid-ers the object as representing a category. Otherwise, he experiences the word as a sound complex belonging to an object. He frequently pronounces the word in the way we pronounce a word of a foreign language, the sound of which we know but which has no definite meaning for us. This difference becomes particularly evident in patients whose speech is not exceptionally impoverished, who have a fairly ample vocabulary and verbal knowledge. Such a patient may be able to bring out many words in relation to objects as a reaction to the question, "What is this or this?" and is also able to describe his intention in uttering the word. As much as it may seem in such cases as if the patient names the object, his description shows clearly that actually he does not.[10]

Categories are relations. The category "red" implies a rela-tion among the various shades of red as well as a relation to other categories of color. When we become conscious of the meaning of a word and understand it, our understanding of the word, our subjective sense of it, is of the relations that constitute its meaning. Thus what Goldstein calls the "concrete" use of a word by a patient reveals the patient's restricted sense of the relations that the word usually suggests. He may be able to use a word in a specific setting, but the restricted subjectivity of this use is shown by his inability to understand the word alone and isolated. His subjective world lacks abstract relations to his surroundings, and so, inevitably, words lose their abstract meaning:

> How very concretely such words are taken may be demonstrated by another example. When to such a patient a knife was offered, together with a pencil, she called the knife a "pencil sharpener"; when the knife was offered with an apple, it was to her an "apple parer"; in company with a piece of bread, it became a "bread knife" and together with a fork it was a "knife and fork." The word knife alone she never uttered spontaneously and when she was asked, "Could we not always call it simply knife?," she replied promptly, "No."[11]

Thus naming is more than making categories: it is establishing relations among objects or people and oneself. For as Goldstein notes, his patients may refuse to use the word "red" though they have no difficulty saying the sound "red." *Forced* to use it, one of his patients said: "I said it because you wanted me to." Or another, when forced to arrange fabrics by color, said, "It's not that at all. It is completely false!"[12] What she probably meant was not very different from what Sacks meant when he called his leg "alien" or other patients meant when they said they had "counterfeit" arms or legs. These patients can no longer use certain words in a meaningful sense because, self-reference having been lost, the words have become "false." Goldstein's patient can categorize colors in relation to the clothes she is wearing but not in relation to an abstract color entity, because the latter has lost meaning, since she can no longer relate it to *her*. Patients with aphasia who can repeat words but not use them (a common occurrence) have lost self-reference for the categories those words represent. The words seem "false" in the sense that Sacks's leg was "alien"; the aphasic's words are like alien objects.

Meaning and understanding, then, are self-referential—they emerge from self-reference and are structured in terms of it. Changes in subjectivity, changes in the frame of reference, alter meanings and knowledge in general. A patient whose subjective state is what Gelb and Goldstein call "concrete" cannot understand words abstractly. The meaning of a word derives initially from an individual's subjective world; it is never absolute; it has a direct relation to the person's body image and the use of that image to achieve various physical goals. A more abstract sense of meaning requires a more abstract sense of body image and its relations to actions. I can establish a common ground and some mutual understanding with you through language because we can grasp each other's utterances and actions as meaning something in terms of our own subjective worlds and what we abstract from them; other people's thoughts and actions relate to our private worlds in ways that are similar, but not identical, to our own ways of trying to come to grips with inevitably similar experiences. When we all call a given person "Ezra" we are referring to the same person though our perceptions of him may differ.

We must recognize that all spoken language, like all mental acts, has self-reference and that the brain mechanisms creating self-reference may, when altered, alter our use of language, just as they may alter our knowledge of our bodies or objects in our surroundings. This is not a mere speculative argument: a careful examination of the neurological evidence makes it, I believe, unavoidable.

Part of the complex structure of categories is that they are built up in the brain, self-referentially, from categories of lesser complexity; recategorization creates more abstract, complex structures. Clinically, as Head noted, the loss of individual words in a brain-damaged patient is never absolute; what remains, as Gelb and Goldstein had argued, too, is a linguistic structure of lesser complexity. As Head puts it:

> It is absurd to say that the patient is "word-deaf" or "word-blind"; for his power of appreciating spoken or written words depends more on the nature and severity of the problems to be solved than on the particular sense to which it is presented. . . . Evidently the hypothesis that the normal use of language is built up out of auditory and visual images is unsupported by experience, and fails to explain the phenomena of so-called "sensory" disorders of speech. . . .

Indeed, speech, or thought in general, is not a combination of words, or even sentences:

> We neither think nor speak in combinations of verbal units. In order to understand the morbid phenomena of speech they must be considered as a disturbance of progressive acts, which cannot reach their proper conclusion. They are not due to disintegration of isolated words strung together in sequence. Not only is it impossible to break up a word into auditory and visual elements, but disease does not analyse a sentence into its verbal or grammatical constit-

uents. We cannot even assume that a sentence is strictly a unit of speech. Speech, like walking, is an act of progression. It is impossible to obtain a satisfactory conception of how a man walks from a single instantaneous photograph; before we can give the impression of motion, the pictures must pass in an unbroken series as through a cinematograph.[13]

Head's views, like those of Gelb and Goldstein, were a challenge to classical neurology's claim that a patient's inability to use certain words was due to a specific memory loss. Yet today the classical arguments have once again regained dominance, in a slightly revised form; the claim is it is not specific words that are lost following brain damage, but rather specific categories of words (colors, foods), certain of which are innately determined. For example, the French psychologists Jacques Mehler and Emmanuel Dupoux have argued that at birth the visual system of the brain "already classifies colors in categories that are similar to those used spontaneously by adults."[14] They note that four-month-old babies, having been exposed to blue for a certain period of time, react when the color is changed to green but not when the new color is a variant of blue. Yet though a child of three and a half years can use words like "big" and "little," it cannot name colors (an ability that comes at about four). This delay in the verbal acquisition of color names, they argue, occurs because the language centers are not connected to the visual centers until later: "the late acquisition of words designating colors in the infant . . . [can be explained by postulating] that the development of these cortical structures is slow and does not occur before the age of four years." These same connections, they say, have been destroyed or damaged in patients like those of Gelb and Goldstein who cannot name colors that they nevertheless perceive: these patients have suffered "a break in the nerve connections that link the structures in the cerebral cortex that subserve the function of vision to those that permit language." The language centers have been disconnected from the visual centers that create the innate categories of colors, which "explains the similar performance of the child and the patient."[15]

Yet the study of Gelb and Goldstein's patient suggests, on the contrary, that "red" is *not* an innate category: their patient fails to put different shades of red, which she can nonetheless perceive, together in one category. The generalizing word "red" has no meaning for her because she does not see any relations among its various shades: she finds puzzling Gelb and Goldstein's insistence that all the variant shades are "red."

Similarly, the evidence does not warrant the argument that an infant considers the different shades of a particular color as part of the same category. When a four-and-a-half-month-old infant appears to respond (nonverbally) to a change of color from blue to green while not reacting to changes within the blue category, this does not mean that the infant's brain has classified all the blues together; rather, it is reacting to gross *changes* in the stimulus. Shades of one color (such as different blues) represent rather small changes in the wavelength of light. The eye has only three types of color receptors that are sensitive to wavelengths within the red, green, and blue spectrum, and their sensitivity overlaps. So the change from blue to green, for example, causes a significantly different pattern of activity in the receptors than the change from one blue to another. And it is these significant changes in the patterns of activity of the color receptors that would cause the infant's response.

Even the adult's mature visual system is sensitive to

changes of stimuli, not to their absolute quality. A person who is wearing a red suit and is standing in a room that is furnished and painted entirely in the same red will, eventually, begin to see all the things in that room as a kind of gray. The brain creates qualities—the colors, sounds, and other sensations we are conscious of—by establishing relations *among* stimuli. If all light were the same wavelength, we would know only a gray world. It is therefore very difficult to test whether an infant is aware of different shades of a single color. It seems more probable that before the brain can make the discriminations of variant shades, it first acquires the ability to discriminate the grosser patterns of change that represent the boundaries between colors.

In truth, the categorizations we normally create for colors, as for other categories of stimuli, are abstractions that require language. That all shades of a color form a group is not an inherent characteristic of the visual stimuli themselves; indeed, they are not grouped in like manner in all languages. The Eskimos, for example, have some twenty different expressions for different visual qualities of snow; the Danis of New Guinea have only two categories of colors.[16] In the same way, notions of "big" and "little" that a child appears to acquire at about the age of three and a half are not inherent characteristics of the stimuli but abstractions that are only possible with, and that necessitate, words. For sure, even without any language, one's action may suggest that one can discriminate size, but the idea of size as an abstraction can be represented only with words. That a child is able to use words about size at three and a half years and names for colors only some six months later suggests that the idea of color is more abstract than that of size. The process of categorization, of abstraction and generalization, builds on itself. The highest forms of abstraction require language, but even linguistic forms build on themselves; before we can understand a three-dimensional world we must have mastered a world of two dimensions, and a child masters size ("big" and "little") before it can master color ("red," "green," etc.). This is not because the visual center and the language center were not earlier "connected," nor is it because of the "disconnection" of these centers that Gelb and Goldstein's patient cannot name colors.[17] The *linguistic* category of "red" is considerably more abstract than that of "big" or "little." Learning complex relations requires first learning simple ones. This might explain why it is most unlikely that we can retain infantile or very early childhood memories. It is only when linguistic structure attains a certain complexity that "memory" becomes truly possible.

The pattern of acquisition of language—like our acquisition of perceptual abilities in general—suggests that it depends on the fundamental brain function: creating generalizations or, in a broad sense, establishing relations. And an integral part of linguistic generalization is its conscious, subjective character. That children first learn the words for size and only later the words for colors is an example of the increasing complexity of the process of generalization. Indeed, the development of linguistic skills in general—notably the acquisition of grammar—is itself a perfect example of the process. Learning a language might well be described as the acquisition of the skill of generalization or categorization: "No acquisitional task puts greater demand on children's skill at categorizing than learning to talk. The forms of language are themselves categories, and these forms are linked to a vast network of categorical distinctions in meaning and discourse function."[18]

A child's first utterances, for example, are single words or word-like sounds that bear a categorical relation to certain objects, people, and actions. They are usually overextended in their reference ("doggie" for all four-legged animals), meanings shift, and then new words are invented and subsequently abandoned.[19] At around eighteen to twenty months of age, the child begins to sense the "symbolic" function of words, no longer assuming that they are part of the objects or people they designate. Grammatical structures—different tenses of verbs, single and plural nouns, prepositions, and so on—begin to appear along with two-word utterances. Subsequently, the two-word utterances are strung together with "and," and finally longer simple sentences are produced. The child can distinguish "cat pushes truck" from "truck pushes cat." The child's emerging recognition of his relation to objects, paralleled by his recognition of his relation to others, is reflected in his growing linguistic skills. Children first learn "me" and "you"; later they learn "he," "she," "it," and "they"; observing relations *among* others is more abstract than observing relations of one's own, since one must abstract from self-reference, and the latter is only implicit in one's observation of relations among others.[20] So the increasing complexity of the child's utterances expresses the child's greater understanding of abstract relations.

This pattern of development is similar in all children learning a language—studies have been done in English, and related patterns have been observed in many other languages. There are subtle differences in the pattern of a blind child's acquisition of language, however. Since he is unable to grasp visually the relations between objects and people, the blind child's utterances do not become overextended. Seeing children are eventually able to describe events from many vantage points, but the blind child's utterances are always from the vantage point of the self. Whereas the seeing child's vocabulary suddenly increases at around eighteen months of age, blind children increase their vocabulary steadily but gradually, and they do not invent their own words. Yet being aware of events only after they have happened (John rolls a ball to the child, and the child knows it was rolled only after touching it), they talk about the past before seeing children do.[21] They establish contact with others based on a shared past. Distinguishing past and present events may be one of the important ways in which blind children recognize the abstract relations that make up events and that are embedded in the linguistic structures we use to describe them.

Seeing children, then, understand some aspects of the symbolic nature of language relatively early, for they have learned to generalize non-self-referentially about relations among people and objects. A blind child has greater difficulty doing this. The seeing child's large vocabulary incorporates these complex relations into memories—not memories in the sense of stored images, but memory as an ability to understand and sustain complex relations. The child's utterances begin to have a symbolic character; given his new ability to abstract, a larger vocabulary becomes useful and understandable. The blind child of the same age does not yet have this abstracting ability, and his slightly slower acquisition of words goes along with a memory that is not so complex; different strategies (a more vivid sense of past versus present; a greater dependency on the mother's language) permit him eventually to develop a complex memory.

Both blind and seeing children develop their linguistic skills by categorizing and recategorizing their own and adult language in terms of their conceptual development, and this depends at first on bodily explorations of their surroundings. As language becomes symbolic, it becomes part of that conceptual development. Insofar as adult usage is beyond a child's conceptual grasp, the child will ignore it and use only what fits into his conceptual world. The adult model both constrains and expands the child's awareness of his surroundings.[22]

Consciousness is a continuum. As Head noted, we can describe our posture only in relation to what it has been. We can "know" only in relation to what we "knew" a few moments ago. A conscious awareness is of neither the old nor the immediate but of a transformation and conflation of both. Language, too, has meaning in relation to what we knew a few moments ago. A child's linguistic evolution—from overextended syllables to two-word utterances and finally to sentences—is an individual history of consciousness, where language expresses, then becomes a part of and even helps determine, the child's awareness of the world. The blind child's perceptual world evolves along with his linguistic world. They are as closely related as a sighted child's world is related to his sense of movement and touch.

Children deprived of human contact never learn to speak, and their awareness of the world must therefore be quite different from that of youngsters who have been more fortunate. On the other hand, children who have contact with their peers but lack an adult model of language will learn to gesticulate and babble among themselves, and they will categorize these gesticulations and babblings into a form of communication we might call "gestural" language. But lacking an adult model, this will not develop into a true language, with symbols and a fully developed grammar. Normal children can, over time, abstract the symbolic and grammatical nature of language from adult speech. Without such a model, children have to create the notions of a grammar and symbols among themselves; and the process of abstracting (or recategorizing) gestures into symbols, and relations among symbols into grammar, is very long. Generalized linguistic patterns take several years to emerge, and they cannot, evidently, do so after puberty. In fact, it is impossible for one generation of children to accomplish the task; only a second generation, whose model is the "gestural" language invented by their older comrades, can create a true grammatical language with symbols. One generation is building on, abstracting from, the behavior of the previous one. The complex process of abstracting and categorizing, and the limits of time, make it impossible for more developed grammatical forms to emerge when "babbling" is the only model of "language." Language learning is a slow process. Many different kinds of abstraction and category—both examples of establishing relations—must develop.

This long process of abstracting, or categorizing, from babbling (or, in the second generation, from gestures) creates language. There are not, as some claim, innate neural structures that are specific for language, for if there were, why would babbling children, who have no other linguistic models, fail to develop true grammatical languages with symbols? Why is a second generation needed? It is difficult to reconcile this two-stage pattern, as well as the normal pattern of language acquisition I have already described, with claims that there are innate structures in the brain specific for language. During evolution, the development of larger brains, along with the muscular ability to make complicated vocal gestures or hand movements, led to an increased capacity to generalize and abstract from the mutual interaction of gestural patterns; true grammatical and symbolic language did not develop spontaneously but required at least two generations to emerge.

The two-stage pattern can be observed in a number of ways. For example, deaf children brought up by parents who know no sign language will develop a gestural language. One study describes the gesturing among the deaf children in these terms:

> The children developed two types of signs to refer to objects and actions. First, they used deictic signs, typically pointing gestures which, like proforms in English (such as "this" or "there"), effectively allow the child to make reference to any object or person in the present. However, . . . context is necessary to interpret these signs. . . . The children pro-

duced a second type of sign, characterizing signs, which are motor-iconic signs that specify actions, objects and less frequently, attributes. For example, a closed fist bobbed in and out near the mouth referred to a banana or to the act of eating a banana. Two hands flapped up and down at shoulder height referred to a bird or the act of flying. . . . In addition to these lexical acocmplishments, the children concatenated their deictic and characterizing signs into multisign phrases that conveyed relations between objects and actions. For example, one child pointed at a shoe and then pointed at a table to request that the shoe . . . be put on the table.[23]

This first-generation gestural language can be enriched over time, but it cannot develop into a true sign language with symbols and fully developed grammar, because, as I have said, linguistic ability (that is, the acquisition of more complicated gestural patterns or complete syntax) does not evolve after puberty. However, younger deaf children with no exposure to sign language will, if brought into the company of gestural signers, develop a true sign language. In England, for example, when signing was forbidden in schools for the deaf and students were forced to imitate spoken languages, the students nonetheless developed a gestural sign language, signing to each other behind the backs of their teachers. Younger students, noticing these exchanges, began to sign among themselves as well and developed a full grammatical language, with a syntax equivalent to those of modern sign languages. That is, younger deaf children abstract (categorize) the gestures of older students, creating from them symbols and more abstract categories of relations among these symbols—a true grammar. An older child may point (gesture) to a rabbit to indicate his subject; the younger one will categorize the pointing gesture as "rabbit," and the gesture becomes a symbol. The relational patterns of the gestures are then abstracted into a grammar, and the ambiguity of the symbol is eliminated as the child expands his vocabulary.

A similar pattern has been observed in the development of creole from pidgin languages. Pidgin languages arise when immigrant workers from various linguistic backgrounds are forced to create a system of communication in their common second language. Pidgin is similar to gestural sign language in that its grammar is primitive or nonexistent. (For example, "Building high place wall part now-time and then now-temperature every time give you" means "There is a sign high up on the wall that will show you the time and temperature right now."[24]) Children of pidgin speakers develop a creole language, abstracting or recategorizing the pidgin of their parents, just as deaf students recategorize the gestures of older students. Creole speakers in Hawaii have no contact with creole speakers in Jamaica or the Seychelles, but the grammatical structures of their creole languages are remarkably similar. And children's mistakes when acquiring languages other than their "mother tongue" often resemble creole.

Some linguists believe these common features support the view that there are innate biological rules for language. But cultural requirements can account for the common features; and the development of creole from pidgin is analogous to the developmental stages of sign language. These patterns suggest, I believe, the categorical nature of brain function, the incessant creation of relations, not the presence of specific innate rules in the brain.[25]

And categorical brain function accounts as well for the diversity of human languages. This is yet another example of the brain's constant reworking of its own generalizations. The transformation from a gestural form of language to a true grammatical language is on a continuum with the processes of abstraction that created the initial gestural language; it is hardly surprising that these processes should create variant forms of language all over the globe. Language is the ultimate form of subjectivity, a subjectivity that can reflect on itself and on the self's relations to others. *All* forms of subjectivity—including nonlinguistic ones—concern relations between the individual and his surroundings; subjectivity itself is a matter of relation, and so is language. Just as there can be no language in total isolation, so also there can be no consciousness unless the brain establishes relations with its surroundings. What is astonishing about language is that it establishes relations between the subjective worlds of individuals and between the individual *and himself* (the true language phase, which permits self-reflection); grammar is an incidental consequence of this process of abstraction. Like subjectivity and like consciousness in general, language thus develops. To view it as depending on a set of abstract grammatical rules falsifies its very nature; it is part of the very structure of consciousness.

If language is categorizing, then its emergence in evolution did not require the development of a special "language organ." Rather, following a considerable increase in brain size and the development of a vocal apparatus, the hominid ancestors of humans, and humans too, became capable of producing complicated vocal and hand gestures. A special memory system appeared that categorized the vocal cords' gestural patterns. The brain, linking these gestures to its nonlinguistic categorizations of its own activities, and categorizing these linked signals in another special memory system, created the basis for a gestural system that can refer to objects and actions. A developed gestural language became a stimulus and was recategorized into symbols and a true syntax. After sufficient lexical experience, the language was in turn treated as a stimulus by the categorical centers and recategorized; thus language became an independent means of thought, creating the notion of time past, present, and future.

Language appeared, then, when complicated gesturing became possible with the vocal cords and the hands, and when an enlarged brain (Broca's and Wernicke's areas and the connecting fibers) could categorize this gestural production. The gesturing of the vocal cords or of the hands became a dynamic frame of reference, and hence a part of (and essential to) language, just as the dynamic body image is the frame of reference and a part of (and essential to) direct visual perception.

An individual's utterances have meaning only in terms of his total articulatory capacities. It is the breakdown of this articulatory capacity, in Broca's aphasia, for example, that limits the patient's ability to express himself and to understand others. And it is the isolation of these articulatory structures from other brain functions, as in Wernicke's aphasia, that destroys self-reference, making speech "incoherent" and comprehension impossible. Words become "alien." In normal linguistic development, the complexity of the articulatory structures that a child acquires depends, as we have seen, on the models he is exposed to.

This idea of linguistic development—of language evolving from a "gestural" to a "symbolic" form—gives a neurophysiological basis to some modern linguistic arguments. It is at odds, however, with the claim that language is based on genetically determined innate structures acting according to very specific rules. As already mentioned, genes cannot determine the fine-branching structure of nerve cells and it is therefore difficult to imagine how any rules could be embedded in the brain; since brain responses occur in response to unpredictable environmental stimuli that have no predetermined meaning in themselves, they are best understood as representing categorizations of stimuli. Indeed, as I have said, one alleged piece of evidence for innate rules of language—that the enormous variety of human languages may be based on certain fundamental rules known as a universal grammar—is perhaps better seen as evidence for the categorizing nature of brain function. For not only are the basic gestural patterns used in language limited, but the prelinguistic categorizations to which they are linked are very broad discriminatory ones that allow the brain to establish relations among objects and actions.

The idea of a universal grammar is not new. An early nineteenth-century proponent was the German philosopher Wilhelm von Humboldt (1767–1835), whose work was ignored by the diagram makers but who greatly influenced Gelb and Goldstein. Humboldt spoke of the "form of language," by which he meant the larger structure of which individual languages are a part:

> The concept of the form of languages extends far beyond the rules of *word-order* and even beyond those of *word-formation*. Insofar as we mean by these the application of certain general logical categories, of active and passive, substance, attribute, etc. to the roots and basic words, it is quite applicable to the formation of the *basic words* themselves, and must in fact be applied to them as much as possible, if the nature of language is to be truly recognizable.

For him, all languages were an expression of a more general linguistic structure or form: "Through exhibiting the form we must perceive the specific course which the language . . . has hit upon for the *expression of thought*. We must be able to see how it relates to other languages. . . . In its own nature it is itself an apprehension of particular *linguistic elements in mental unity.*[26]

More recently, Noam Chomsky has stated a similar position, replacing the idea of "form" with "universal grammar":

> The study of universal grammar . . . is the study of the nature of human intellectual capacities. It tries to formulate the necessary and sufficient conditions that a system must meet to qualify as a potential human language, conditions that are not accidentally true of the existing human languages, but that are rooted in the human "language capacity," and thus constitute the innate organization that determines what counts as linguistic experience and what knowledge of language arises on the basis of this experience.[27]

Chomsky goes on to make a clear-cut distinction between the innate rules responsible for a particular mental function (such as language) and memory: "language is rule-governed not memory-produced behavior."[28] A child learning a language may have "the knowledge of the appropriate rules and forms," "but for some reason lacked the capacity to use it; . . . perhaps because of limits on memory."[29] In his view, the rules of language are unlike the rules governing other mental functions, and memory, whatever role it may play in a given mental function, is clearly a separate "system":

> There seems little reason to suppose, for the moment, that there are general principles of cognitive structure, or even of human cognition, expressible at some higher level, from which the particular properties of particular "mental organs," such as the language faculty, can be deduced, or even that there are illuminating analogies among these various

systems. Of course, we do expect to find that some systems—say, the systems of memory—enter into a variety of cognitive processes, but that is another matter altogether.[30]

Humboldt's position is more ambiguous. While he glosses over the question of memory, he suggests that linguistic capacities are acquired over time, recategorizing, as it were, what has already been learned:

The *speech-learning* of children is not an assignment of words, to be deposited in memory and rebabbled by rote through the lips, but a growth in linguistic capacity with age and practice. What is heard does more than merely convey information to oneself; it readies the mind also to understand more easily what has not yet been heard; it makes clear what was long ago heard, but then half understood, or not at all, in that a similarity to the new perception suddenly brings light to the power that has since become sharpened; and it enhances the urge and capacity to absorb from what is heard ever more, and more swiftly, into the memory, and to let ever less of it rattle by as mere noise.[31]

This passage suggests the idea of a universal grammar, and indeed Humboldt speaks of "laws of production." What is interesting is that his "laws of production" are also consistent with a categorical view. One can read Humboldt as one likes: he influenced both Chomsky and the very different school of thought of Gelb and Goldstein. For example, he writes:

The picture of language as designating merely *objects*, already perceived in themselves, is also disconfirmed by examination of what language engenders as its product. By means of such a picture we would never, in fact, exhaust the deep and full content of language. Just as no concept is possible without language, so also there can be no object for the mind, since it is only through the concept, of course, that anything external acquires full being for consciousness.

And if there is a suggestion that language acquisition is recategorical, it is also self-referent, or subjective, like all perceptual activities:

> the whole mode of *perceiving* things *subjectively* necessarily passes over into cultivation and the use of language. For the *word* arises from this very perceiving; it is a copy not of the object in itself, but of the image thereof produced in consciousness. Since all objective perception is inevitably tinged with *subjectivity*, we may consider every human individual, even apart from language, as a unique aspect of the world-view.[32]

Indeed, the subjectivity of language, its self-referential quality, is implicit in the claim that it is categorical, for categories are derived from individual experience. The categories are memory, and therefore the rules that emerge from categorization describe the process of memory.

Chomsky's distinction between "rule-governed" and "memory-produced" behavior is misleading, for they are both descriptions of the same process. It is a distinction not unlike that of the nineteenth-century neurologists who thought memory images were stored in specialized (preprogrammed) brain centers. But on the contrary, memory-produced behavior must be categorical behavior, and it must be self-referential. *All conscious behavior is categorizing and self-referential.* Linguistic behavior, too, is conscious behavior, and it, too, must have the structural characteristics of consciousness I have been discussing. The ways in which categories are created can be described in terms of rules; and the rules that emerge in different cognitive domains (visual, linguistic, etc.) will differ, but the process (self-referential categorization) is always the same. The reason the brain creates one set of categories rather than another has to do with the nature of the stimuli, the past experience of the individual, and the constraints of the body's needs and potential actions. Self-reference is an integral part of the process. Over time, actions may acquire a certain regularity, which can be described using rules. But one should not confuse the rules with actual brain processes. Arguments for a universal grammar bear an uncanny resemblance to the claims of the Preformationists of the eighteenth century, who tried to explain the complexity of the newborn infant's body by saying that its complex form must have been present from the start in the sperm and egg. So, too, some linguists insist, grammar must be preprogrammed in our brains, or we could never acquire it. This only confuses the end result with the processes that create it. In fact, there is something terribly misleading about the idea of innate rules and innate grammar. As the English philosopher and historian R. C. Collingwood once wrote:

We vaguely suppose it [grammar] to be a science; we think that the grammarian, when he takes a discourse and divides it into parts, is finding out the truth about it, and that when he lays down rules for the relations between these parts he is telling us how people's minds work when they speak. This is very far from being the truth. A grammarian is not a kind of scientist studying the actual structure of language; he is a kind of butcher, converting it from organic tissue into marketable and edible joints. Language as it lives and grows no more consists of verbs, nouns, and so forth than animals as they live and grow consist of forehands, gammons, rump steaks, and other joints.[33]

It is not surprising that the kinds of processes that gave rise to consciousness in the first place are responsible for the creation of language as well. Words and sentences are the source and staple of the mental images of higher consciousness. And just as the nonlinguistic mental images in consciousness transform an irretrievable, individual past and present, words and sentences, too, have an irretrievable history, which differs for every individual. The significance of words or sentences depends on an accumulated experience, as well as the immediate context, and the mental images based on them transform both. The mental image created in nonlinguistic consciousness and that created by language are thus analogous; they represent two different ways of transforming history and the present. For sure, language creates infinitely richer combinations, but it is an elaboration of the same fundamental principles that gave rise to the first conscious mental image. During evolution, new areas of the brain developed, not new principles of mental function. Language added an explicit form of self-reference; humans are conscious of themselves as opposed to others. The notions of "I," "you," and "the other" emerged, and with them the possibility that the self could be "multiple personalities."

V

Multiple Personalities:
What's in a Name?

We change over time, yet we *know*, we *feel*, we are always the same person. "Wisdom," "maturity," "growth," are ways of describing our sense of the past as well as our sense of the present. We can "have regrets," do what is "out of character"; these expressions acknowledge that the regrettable or peculiar acts were our own. We can describe ourselves as having many personalities, but the very effort belies our sense of unity; the subtle or not so subtle variations in our personalities are an essential part of our unified sense of self.

Ultimately, our feeling of oneness, of being a single unique person, cannot be separated from our sense that we have a name, just as our awareness of the thing called redness cannot be separated from the single word "red." We are our names. We give names to abstractions—persons, qualities, and things, including ourselves—and this act of naming reveals the brain's ability to create an abstract relation it grasps independently of its immediate awareness of its surroundings. We can learn to cross the street on the green and stop on the red even if we have no language; but without language we would have no idea that red and green are examples of a quality—

an abstraction—that can be called "color." Our ability to know the *idea* of color requires some kind of symbolic representation, such as a word; without it there is no sense in which we can be said to know that "color" exists.

The act of naming, then, reflects our understanding of a kind of relation—of an abstraction—that can exist (even in an imaginary sense), that we can be aware of, that we can know. Brain damage may limit this awareness; Gelb and Goldstein's patient who considered the word "red" false was brain damaged in a way that kept her from understanding the abstract idea of a group of colors of varying shades.

Similarly, the notion of selfhood is encapsulated in a name. And like patients with neurological disorders that prevent them from naming categories of colors, there are patients who lose their sense of being one person. The patient cannot understand that his different selves are all one, and this may be because one "self" lacks the sense of pain and the other or others do not. Like an "alien" leg, the self deprived of the sense of pain cannot seem to belong to a person who in some respects *does* feel pain; so that first "self" must be given another name. Having several names is characteristic of patients with the disorder of "multiple personalities."

That in such patients one self seems to alternate with one or several others shows the absence of a unified sense of a single person in a single body. The individual personalities within a multiple personality seem to pick up where the others leave off; when Ansel becomes Arthur, he knows or remembers nothing of Ansel and continues as if he had been Arthur all along: whatever happened to Ansel is forgotten. Likewise for Ansel, who knows nothing of Arthur. The single, bodily brain appears to be generating separate personalities, separate collections of memories.

Cases of multiple personalities are a perfect example of

what the classical neurologists were talking about when they spoke of accessibility or inaccessibility of memory images; multiple personalities were caused, they thought, by a temporary inaccessibility of memories that were the crucial unifying elements of a personality. William James expressed this view when he wrote:

> Alternating personality in its simplest phases seems based on lapses of memory. Any man becomes, as we say, *inconsistent* with himself if he forgets his engagements, pledges, knowledges, and habits; and it is merely a question of degree at what point we shall say that his personality is changed. In the pathological cases known as those of double or alternate personality the lapse of memory is abrupt, and is usually preceded by a period of unconsciousness or syncope lasting a variable amount of time.[1]

These conclusions are, however, hasty. What appeared to James as lapses of memory may be the brain structuring "memory" in response to stimuli in different ways. When Arthur does not remember what Ansel did, this does not mean that there is stored in the brain a fixed record of Ansel's activities, which Arthur has lost and which will reappear when he transforms back into Ansel, any more than there is a dictionary of all the words I know stored in my brain, waiting for me to use them. I create my language, and my sense of myself, more dynamically, just as I move around bodily in space. My sense of "posture" is not stored in my brain, but, rather, the ability to create one posture from another is, the ability to establish relations. And the senses of self and speech, like posture, are constantly evolving structures; what I just said determines, in part, what I will say. Just as one posture gives rise to another and one sentence gives rise to another, one expression of my personality gives rise to another.

Memory, too, comprises the acquired habits and abilities for organizing postures and sentences—for establishing relations. So there is no "Ansel" organized as such in "Arthur's" brain, or vice versa. Rather, the single brain organizes itself as if it were Ansel (and there had never been an Arthur), then vice versa, because under certain circumstances this damaged brain is reorganizing its way of responding to stimuli, the nature of its relations with the world.* That the brain can undergo such apparently profound reorganization shows not that some memories are forgotten and others suddenly recalled (for what would be the basis of the appropriate relevancy?) but, on the contrary, that the brain can establish new relations, can alter points of view in ways that alter the very nature of what we call "memory"—the act of remembering. This truth, after all, is part of an ordinary person's everyday psychology. Yesterday's "friend" is today's "objectionable person."

Indeed, we might say that in one sense the multiple personality is a patient who has too few selves. None of his or her personalities fully "fits" the dynamic experience of everyday life. Pathology has limited the responses and therefore the dynamic, ever-changing nature of self: one personality will recognize family and friends; another will treat them as strangers and enemies. These multiple personalities can be remarkably similar to the neurological cases we have discussed.

Typical is the case of Mary Reynolds, one of the earliest

*Much has been written about patients who appear to have "knowledge without awareness." Individuals, for example, with a disorder known as prosopagnosia are unable to recognize the familiar faces of people such as their own family and friends. Nonetheless, some of these patients had galvanic skin responses when shown photographs of family and friends whom they otherwise could not identify, a bodily response that is taken neurologically to be an example of "knowledge without awareness."[2] In its diminished state, the brain is in these cases limited to the galvanic response to the photographs. But this is not exactly "knowledge," though some bodily reference remains, and it does not suggest that anything else is going on in the patient's brain in response to the pictures. Knowledge is the brain's ability to organize itself in particular ways at particular times.

studies of a multiple personality, which William James discussed at length in his *The Principles of Psychology*.[3] Mary Reynolds was born in England and was still a child when her family moved to the relatively uninhabited countryside of Titusville, Pennsylvania. There this "dull and melancholy young woman" lived an apparently uneventful life, until, at about nineteen, she was found lying unconscious in the woods. She eventually recovered consciousness, but she remained blind and deaf for some six weeks. Three months later, she was again found in a state of profound sleep from which it was impossible to wake her. Some twenty hours later she awakened; now her memory was gone. She was like a newborn infant: "To all intents and purposes she was being for the first time ushered into the world. All of the past that remained to her was the faculty of pronouncing a few words, and this seems to have been as purely instinctive as the wailings of an infant. . . . Her eyes were for the first time opened upon the world. Old things had passed away; all things had become new." A few weeks later, she had again "learned" to speak, read, and write. But she did not recognize her parents, brothers, sisters, or friends, and claimed she had never seen them before, "never known them—was not aware that such persons had been." She was meeting them for the first time. "To the scenes by which she was surrounded she was a perfect stranger." She never learned to accept her relation to her family and friends.

Yet—and this is most significant—she was hardly troubled by the peculiarity of her circumstances. She was a young woman who knew neither her parents nor her origins and who had not the slightest idea how she had wound up in a household of strangers; yet these matters were of no concern to her because in her mental world—a world without any personal history, with no names, with no chronology about people she knew and saw daily—they were of no significance or sense. "She considered those she had once known as for the most part strangers and enemies, among whom she was, by some remarkable and unaccountable means, transplanted, though from what region or state of existence was a problem unsolved."

Her normal taciturn and unimaginative personality was gone:

Instead of being melancholy she was now cheerful to extremity. Instead of being reserved she was buoyant and social. Formerly taciturn and retiring, she was now merry and jocose. Her disposition was totally and absolutely changed. While she was in this second state, extravagantly fond of company, she was much more enamored of nature's works. . . . She used to start in the morning, either on foot or horseback, and ramble until nightfall over the whole country; nor was she at all particular whether she were on a path or in the trackless forest. Her predilection for this manner of life may have been occasioned by the restraint necessarily imposed upon her by her friends, which caused her to consider them her enemies, and not companions, and she was glad to keep out of their way.

Mary Reynolds had become fearless, much as if she had lost the sense of pain. Indeed, in her "second state" she bears an uncanny resemblance to Madame I, who had no sense of pain and said that her family appeared phantom-like; to Babinski's patients; and to Oliver Sacks when his anesthetized, paralyzed limb appeared "alien" or "counterfeit." And yet unlike these patients, she did not complain that what she saw and recognized was false. Sacks's leg seemed alien to him because he was viewing his anesthetized leg from the point of view of a self that knew pain. People, or parts of the body, become alien, phantom-like, or counterfeit when they can, in some sense, be recognized but when their relation to the observer, the self, has changed—when they do not "belong" to him. Mary Reynolds as her "second self" had no basis on which she could relate to the person she had been, and everything she experienced was transformed by the new perspective. "Alien" and "counterfeit" imply a unified self; Mary Reynolds now had two different selves. Lacking fear and a sense of personal history, her "second self" possessed a knowledge and an understanding of the world that were entirely different from what they had been. She saw, for example, fearsome bears as harmless black hogs:

She knew no fear, and as bears and panthers were numerous in the woods, and rattlesnakes and copperheads abounded everywhere, her friends told her of the danger to which she exposed herself, but it produced no other effect than to draw a contemptuous laugh, as she said, "I know you only want to frighten me and keep me at home, but you miss it, for I often see your bears and I am perfectly convinced that they are nothing more than black hogs."

One evening, after her return from her daily excursion, she told the following incident: "As I was riding to-day along a narrow path a great black hog came out of the woods and stopped before me. I never saw such an impudent black hog before. It stood up on its hind feet and grinned and gnashed its teeth at me. I could not make the horse go on. I told him he was a fool to be frightened at a hog, and tried to whip him past, but he would not go on and wanted to turn back. I told the hog to get out of the way, but he did not mind me. "Well," said I, "if you won't for words, I'll try blows"; so I got off and took a stick and walked up toward it. When I got pretty close by, it got down on all fours and walked away slowly and sullenly, stopping every few steps and looking back and grinning and growling. Then I got on my horse and rode on.

The fearless Mary Reynolds saw growling bears as grinning black hogs. So, too, I might find a menacing person's tantrums silly and comical; only if I feared the person would his clowning become menacing. What I recognize and remember and what makes sense to me are relationships, which then help to form my sense of self. Fear, like all the emotions, shapes the self and ultimately the nature of recognition. Subtle changes in personality, variations in my emotional reactions, will alter my relation to my surroundings.

The loss of self-reference in Madame I, Babinski's patients, and Oliver Sacks occasioned a breakdown of emotional organization and hence of self and memory. Madame I saw phantom-like images of her family members; Sacks saw an alien limb; Mary Reynolds saw "strangers." The change in self, the different point of reference, has restructured memory and, consequently, recognition; a brain response that for one self meant "bears" for another meant "black hogs." Memory is a conscious image structured in terms of the self. Indeed, all forms of perceiving (seeing, touching, and hearing)—even of people, places, or things we have never encountered before—are forms of remembering; the ways in which we make sense of and understand what we see, touch, or hear are determined by our accumulated experience. In her timeless, fearless state, her "second self," Mary Reynolds perceived the world differently; this is symptomatic of as profound a change in brain function as those changes undergone by Madame I or by Babinski's patients. When her brain function changed, so did the point of reference and the nature of the self; so, too, did the nature and structure of memory. In her "fearless" state, Mary Reynolds had a limited range of reactions; when her sense of fear returned, she was also limited in her responses, being generally melancholic: she had "too much" fear. Normally one's responses to people and surroundings are more varied and more dynamic; a normal person in this sense has many "personalities." Mary Reynolds had only two: a "fearless," reckless one and a melancholic, depressive one.

Thus it continued for five weeks, when one morning, after a protracted sleep, she awoke and was herself again. She recognized the parental, the brotherly, and sisterly ties as though nothing had happened. . . . Nature bore a different aspect. Not a trace was left in her mind of the giddy scenes through which she had passed. Her ramblings through the forest, her tricks and humor, all were faded from her memory, and not a shadow left behind. Her parents saw her child; her brothers and sisters saw their sister. She now had all the knowledge that she had possessed in her first state previous to her change. . . . Of course her natural disposition returned; her melancholy was deepened by the information of what had occurred. . . . After the lapse of a few weeks she fell into a profound sleep, and awoke in her second state, taking up her new life again precisely where she had left it.

With her change of self, her knowledge, the *structure* of her memory—the nature of remembering—changed too. "All the knowledge she possessed was that acquired during the few weeks of her former period of second consciousness. She knew nothing of the intervening time." It was not memories that she had lost, repressed, or suppressed. The very nature of her past as a fearless or melancholic person had been transformed.

When she was told of that past from the perspective of other observers, no "memories" were rekindled; the new information was "understood" as only the present ("second") self could understand it: "In this state she came to understand perfectly the facts of her case, not from memory, but from information. Yet her buoyancy of spirits was so great that no depression was produced. On the contrary, it added to her cheerfulness, and was made the foundation, as was everything else, of mirth."

That Mary Reynolds could, at different times, call the same animal a "black hog" or a "bear" suggests how misleading are discussions of memory that fail to distinguish between unconscious "memories" and conscious ones. Conscious processes are dynamic and self-referent; they are relational and never fixed in time. There cannot be unconscious "traces" of these conscious states, since they require a dynamic organization that, given the complexity of the processes (the immediate, the past, and self-reference), are not reproducible. But what *are* more or less reproducible are the ways in which the brain organizes itself; certain pathologies limit the organizational processes, not the accessibility or inaccessibility of memories. When, for example, a patient is unable to say a word but can nonetheless write it, this does not prove that he has a "stored" written form of the word that is intact and another, oral form that has been lost. Failure to elicit a memory is a failure of brain organization. If it were otherwise, the meanings of words would be fixed and language would be a sterile exercise in meaningless repetitions, and this is exactly what language is not; on the contrary, it is the ultimate expression of consciousness. Linguistic deficits must therefore be studied for what they tell us about the dynamics of consciousness. The study of multiple personalities underscores one part of that dynamic, the importance of self. Mary Reynolds was lethargic when melancholic, and full of energy and fearless (probably relatively insensitive to pain) when in her second state. The altered body images were an integral part of her altered "personality" and memory. Neurologically, changes in body image are manifested as distortions of self, changes that make little sense unless the breakdown of memory is taken into account. Though body image is usually not an issue in discussions of multiple-personality cases, it is notable that most of the reported cases, including the ones discussed here, include details about altered bodily functions.

In some cases of multiple personality—cases of "one-way amnesia"—one personality is fully aware of the other. Again, one personality may be "inhibited," serious, and often depressive, and the other gay and freewheeling. While the melancholic personality knows nothing of his or her gay and freewheeling state, the latter knows all about the melancholic states.

Yet the attribution of a past to another personality depends on an extraordinary transformation of body image and point of reference. In 1905 Morton Prince published a study of a Miss Beauchamp, a woman who had

> constant headaches, insomnia, bodily pains, persistent fatigue, and poor nutrition. All of this unfitted her for any work, mental or physical, and even for the amount of exercise that ordinary rules of hygiene required; but in spite of her disability nothing could dissuade her from diligent and, in fact, excessive study which she thought it her duty to persist in.[4]

Prince dubbed Miss Beauchamp "The Saint": "The content of Miss Beauchamp's idea of self was derived from an ideal of perfection inspired by religious teachings and exemplified by the Madonna. . . . Her conception of self included her conception of her relation to Divinity."[5] In contrast, a second personality became evident, Sally, who was full of energy, was fearless, and never slept (she knew Miss Beauchamp's dreams). Prince wrote:

So far as I could see, none of the causes [of fear], such as a thunderstorm, or darkness, or social consequences of conduct, or illness, or fear of inanimate or animate objects, like fire, snakes, spiders, etc., . . . none of these affected Sally. I have known her also to be in the most dangerous situations, such as climbing out on the eaves of the roof and preparing to jump from the fifth story window, without apparently experiencing the slightest fear.[6]

Sally was "totally anesthetic"; she had no sense of pain: "With her eyes closed she can feel nothing. The tactile, pain, thermic, and muscular senses are involved. You may stroke, prick, or burn any part of her skin and she does not feel it. You may place a limb in any posture without her being able to recognize the position which has been assumed." When she looked or listened, however, she could "feel":

But let her open her eyes and look at what you are doing, let her join the visual sense to the tactile or other sense, and the lost sensations at once return. . . . The same is true of auditory perceptions. If Sally hears a sound associated with an object, she can feel the object. For instance, place a bunch of keys in her hand and she does not know what she holds. Now jingle the keys and she can at once feel them.

Yet these recognitions are those of an outsider. She was observing another personality (Miss Beauchamp), much as Babinski's patients and Sacks observed their alien or counterfeit limbs. She seemed divorced from her body image:

Sally's anesthesia extends to the somatic feelings. She is never hungry or thirsty. If she eats she does so as a matter of form or social requirement. There is also an entire absence of bodily discomforts. This anesthesia probably explains in large part Sally's *freedom from ill health*. She does not know the meaning of fatigue, of pain, of ill health. She is always well. . . . Let Miss Beauchamp be suffering from abdominal pain, or headache, or physical exhaustion, and let her change to Sally and at once all these symptoms disappear. Sally knows of the symptoms of the other personalities only through their thoughts or their actions. She does not feel the symptoms themselves. . . . Sally can walk miles without being conscious of the physiological effect. Curiously enough, however, Miss Beauchamp may afterwards suffer from the fatigue effects of Sally's exertions.[7]

With the loss of body image, Sally lost the sense of time as well. Prince wrote:

Most curious is Sally's absolute *ignorance of time*. She cannot compute it. A day, a week, a month are almost the same to her. Things happened "a short time ago," or "a long time ago," in her calendar. But even these expressions do not connote the same ideas to her as to the rest of us. One year is the same as ten years; ten seconds as ten minutes. Ask her to guess a minute, and she is as likely to call time at the end of ten seconds as five minutes.

Sally's notion of self was the abstract self of "long-term memory"; and as with Henri Baud, the structure of her memory, its subjective quality, is difficult to grasp: "It would seem as if time could not be entirely measured by the memory of the succession of events, for Sally experiences events as well as any one else. She does not know her own age."[8] (Freud's description of the unconscious is not unlike this long-term memory as I have been describing it: "The processes of the system *Ucs.* are *timeless*; i.e., they are not ordered temporally, are not altered by the passage of time; they have no reference to time at all. Reference to time is bound up, once again, with the work of the system *Cs.*"[9])

Sally's anesthetic body deprived her of a frame of reference and hence of a sense of time. Blindness, it will be recalled, similarly deprived John Hull, greatly reducing his experience of time. Time is relational, and without a body image, one's temporal relation to the world is inevitably destroyed. And hence the self to which remembered events refer is abstract; one knows that self felt pain or joy, for example, but can no longer really feel that pain or joy except in an abstract way. Miss Beauchamp could feel pain and joy because Miss Beauchamp was a self in contact with, in direct relation to, the immediate world.

Mary Reynolds as a sullen personality was unable to adapt to her surroundings; as a "fearless" personality she was actively able to participate, and she knew nothing of her sullen states. Miss Beauchamp fared no better than the melancholic Mary Reynolds; Sally was like the fearless Mary Reynolds but knew all about Miss Beauchamp, though Sally was numb, anesthetic, an observer of another self.

Physical trauma is the immediate cause of cases of the alien limb; psychological trauma is the cause of multiple personalities. So long as one is conscious of the great pain of a physical trauma, it becomes totally absorbing; self-reference is consumed by it. In certain cases, the brain responds to this crisis by blocking the pain and the associated self-reference of the affected limb. Psychological trauma may similarly first wholly absorb many aspects of self-reference (aspects of "self"), after which the brain blocks the pain and limits the mechanisms of self-reference. A part of the self has disappeared, just as a part of the body disappears in the case of physically traumatized patients with alien limbs. Self-reference and the consequent ability to adapt are lost; pain has engulfed a part of the self.

Great pain divides the self, then, when the brain's process of blocking it absorbs an aspect of self-reference. What might be described as "inhibition" in a "repressed" personality is a loss of aspects of personality, of self-reference. The neurological mechanism of this loss is not the pushing of a traumatic memory into the unconscious but rather a reorganization of the ways in which the brain responds to stimuli. Gelb and Goldstein's patient could not name the color of a red object, not because the word "red" or the idea of "redness" had been repressed, but because his brain could no longer create the structures from which the meaning of the word derived. Sacks's leg had not been repressed; it was that his brain simply could not create a body image that included it. Words like "inhibition" and "repression" are based on notions of memory and brain function that are static, in which the brain's dynamic adaptability—of which human psychology is the best example, after all—is explained by positing discrete dynamic mechanisms. But *all* brain function is dynamic; consciousness itself is a dynamic structure. We should think of "inhibitions" or "repressions" as alterations in the dynamic structure of consciousness, not as separate mechanisms that suddenly come into existence in the face of dangerous or traumatic circumstances.

We understand the present through the past, an understanding that revises, alters, and reworks the very nature of the past in an ongoing, dynamic process. Psychological or physical trauma appears to "fix" memories that may be "released" only years later. That is, the brain isolates painful experiences and removes them from the dynamic process of understanding. What is fixed is not a "memory" but an organizational ability; and what is abnormal is that this breaks the continuity—the dynamic relation with ongoing experience. Not only are the processes that give rise to the traumatic recollections no longer reorganized, but since they are not specific to one episode or another (one "memory" or another), the brain undergoes a new and more general reorganization of its responses to stimuli. The brain cannot block out the pain associated with a given experience without altering its response to other stimuli as well; when a leg becomes alien because the brain is blocking out the enormous pain coming from the damaged limb, space disappears also, though space has nothing to do with the pain. (Pain is blocked by eliminating the mechanisms of self-reference, and this, in turn, destroys the notion of the associated space.) The brain's organizational abilities normally evolve continuously; organizational patterns that are a consequence of trauma become isolated. We acquire habits and patterns of behavior that must be adapted to newer circumstances. But habits associated with trauma cannot be reorganized in appropriate ways, and the brain isolates them: "neurotic" behavior or "multiple personalities" may be a consequence of this faulty reorganization.

The trauma of an accident that causes blindness, for example, can "fix" visual imagery, since the brain can no longer reorganize itself in the face of ongoing visual experience. What in fact have been fixed in this instance, what fail to develop and evolve, are the brain's patterns of organization that produce visual experience. Visual memories then seem out of joint, since they are no longer tied to daily experience, and they cannot be transformed by newer experiences into nonvisual form. Like psychologically traumatic memories, visual images of people with whom the person had no contact after becoming blind remain "visual"; no new organizational patterns cause them to fade out. But images of those with whom the blind person remains in constant contact become transformed by new nonvisual experiences and fade into a new form. Hull, for example, notes:

> It is three years now since I have seen anybody. Strangely enough, I have fairly clear pictures of many people whom I have not met during these three years, but the pictures of the people I have met every day are becoming blurred. . . .
>
> In the case of people I meet every day my relationship has continued beyond the loss of sight, so my thoughts about these people are full of the latest developments in our relationships. These have partly covered the portrait, which has become less important. [The visual images, like habits of thought, have become transformed through continuing contact.] In the case of somebody I know quite well but have not seen for several years, nothing has happened to take the place of the portrait, and when I think of those people, it is the portrait which comes to mind.[10]

The images of people whom the blind person has not encountered are reconstructed with procedures that hardly change with time. He mentally reconstructs old photos: "When I try to conjure up the memory of a loved face, I cannot seem to capture it, but the straight edges of the photograph seem to fix the mobile features firmly in my mind, so that I can imagine myself gazing at the image." But when ongoing encounters are experienced, old photos are no help. Even one's own sense of one's self loses visual meaning. "I find that I am trying to recall old photographs of myself, just to remember what I look like. I discover with a shock that I cannot remember." Hull's new experiences refer now to his nonvisual body image, and inevitably his face "disappears." "Other people have become disembodied voices, speaking out of nowhere, going into nowhere. Am I not like this too, now that I have lost my body?"

In Hull's case, the neurophysiological procedures that once produced visual images have evolved, and they have been transformed by nonvisual procedures in a nonvisual perceptual world: "We do not . . . learn from our own images, nor from our memories," Hull notes incisively, "but only from our perceptions." And further:

> Somehow, it no longer seems important what people look like, or what cities look like. One cannot check at first hand the accuracy of these reports, they lose personal meaning and are relegated to the edge of awareness. They become irrelevant in the conduct of one's life. One begins to live by other interests, other values. One begins to take up residence in another world.[11]*

Beyond this, the world of the blind changes the personal, subjective sense of deep drives and desires—hunger, sex, thirst, for example. For when one is blind, desires, which normally bring forth images of the desired objects, feel as if dissociated from the appropriate images. Hunger and sexual desire become more abstract, less immediate.

> I am often bored by food, feel that I am losing interest in it or cannot be bothered eating. At the same time, I have

---

*The breakdown of old organizational patterns is evident in Hull's failure to remember in which direction the Arabic number 3 points. "I had to trace it with my finger in the air, one, two, three." Once the nonvisual procedures revealed the form of 3, "I remember . . . I also [could not remember] whether the border which goes around the edge of a table cloth or a board is spelt 'border' or 'boarder.' I think I was confused about the board around which there is a border. This illustrates how much the ability to spell is based upon visual images,"[12] indeed, upon ongoing visual experiences in general. Hull's brain had been reorganized, creating new kinds of experiences.

the normal pangs of hunger. Even whilst feeling hungry, I remain unmotivated by the approach of food. I know that it is there because somebody tells me. . . . "But what is it?" I ask. "It's veal cutlet." Now I know. But what do I know? I have this sentence, and I believe it, but the visual cues which excite the actual desire and turn it outwards towards the object are lacking.[13]

So, too, Hull says, sexual desire fails to bring forth the image of the desired person: "The dissociation of desire from image is a very curious and unsettling thing." But is it dissociation, or simply that the brain can't produce the visual images?

In a similar way, trauma in a brain-damaged or psychologically damaged patient causes the memory to have too few "selves," too few personalities. The brain's organizational abilities are limited, making adaptability difficult. In the multiple-personality case, the damaged person shifts from one personality to another, as if searching for a "fit" among a limited number of possibilities where no one personality is good enough. The patient changes personalities much as amnesic aphasics "suddenly 'seize' upon the name of any given object. For among the names that one has proposed to a patient there is only one that relates to the concrete experiences suggested by, or unleashed by, the object."[14] What appear to be different personalities are abrupt changes in the frame of reference (the body image) and, consequently, in "memory" and consciousness in general. Certain organizational patterns create great pain. When the brain blocks the pain, its responses are profoundly reorganized; an "anesthetized" body image alters the nature of recollection and recognition. The patient appears to have a changed personality, for the normal subtle changes and flow of a single integrated and dynamic self have been lost. Of course, we all—at moments of anger, hurt, or joy—get "stuck" in a personality, perhaps unaware of the inappropriateness of our reactions in the circumstances. This normal breakdown of personality has the same emotional, self-referent roots as do the multiple personality or the phenomenon of the "alien" arm or leg.

Failures of memory are structural failures in consciousness, an incapacity to create linguistic or other behavioral responses that are appropriate at a given moment. The inability to establish a flow from one set of structures to another in the case of a multiple personality (from, for example, what Gelb and Goldstein call a "concrete" to a "categorical" attitude) splits and dissociates the self.

Ultimately, self-reference means that a brain must be able to relate itself to a dynamic bodily structure in terms of which stimuli take on meaning, just as words and sentences become meaningful in terms of the dynamic articulatory structures of the vocal apparatus. If the bodily structure is damaged, so is the sense of self, memory, and consciousness. One might imagine reproducing brain functions on a computer, but it is an open question if one could build a sufficiently dynamic "computer body" to which its perceptual mechanisms could refer to enable meaning and understanding to emerge. Part of the extraordinary adaptibility of living things derives from the complexity of the bodies by reference to which their brains create understanding of the world. If we isolate a brain, no matter how sophisticated our techniques, we can never understand its function, because a brain does not function independently of the body it exists in. A brain in a jar is not a brain at all; we can learn some limited things from it, but we must recognize the limitations of that knowledge.

The neurologists' attempts to derive brain function from clinical reports of brain-damaged patients have too often overlooked the fact that the verbal reports of these patients are *conscious* reports. We all use words to convey meaning, to represent our understanding of the world around us. A patient's verbal usage that differs from the normal one is a failure of understanding due to an altered awareness. The patient has had to readjust; his limited awareness causes not the "loss" of words but an inability to make a certain sense of them and thus to use them in conventional ways. Consciousness is dynamic, and memory is part of the dynamics of consciousness.

The clinical evidence must be reexamined, as I have tried to do. For in a concentration on the idea that individual functions had been lost or damaged in brain lesions, important and subtle symptoms went unexplained. Yet these symptoms were part of the patients' *conscious* states, and they suggest a much broader functional breakdown than the view of compartmentalized functions allows. Consciousness is the central issue. Unless we have some idea of what it is all about, we can hardly claim to have understood brain function in general.

In 1926 Henry Head made this very point: "I cannot . . . accept the position of those who deny the existence of consciousness or state that it makes no difference to the ultimate result attained by the response of the organism." When brain damage alters consciousness and consequently the idea of the self, adaptability requires that the brain reorganize the individual's entire relationship to his surroundings. "When some act or process is disturbed in consequence of an organic or functional lesion," Head wrote, "the abnormal response is a fresh integration carried out by all available portions of the central nervous system. It is a total reaction to the new situation. The form assumed by these manifestations cannot be foretold by prior consideration."[15] Consciousness—the dynamic integration of past, present, and self—is the ultimate expression of our individuality. And as we understand more about how it is structured, a new and richer view of brain function and human psychology will begin to emerge.

Notes

I Consciousness

1. Cited in *The Oxford Companion to the Mind*, ed. R. L. Gregory (Oxford, 1987), p. 94. See also Diderot's *Lettre sur les aveugles*, where the work of Molyneux and Cheselden are extensively discussed.

2. Cited in *Oxford Companion*, pp. 94–5.

3. B. Bridgeman, "Intention Itself Will Disappear When Its Mechanisms Are Known," *Behavioral and Brain Sciences* 13 (4 Dec. 1990): 598.

4. See R. G. Mazzolini, "Schemes and Models of the Thinking Machine (1662–1762)," in *The Enchanted Loom: Chapters in the History of Neuroscience*, ed. P. Corsi (New York, 1991), pp. 68–83.

5. Francis Schiller, "Franz Gall (1758–1828)," in Webb Haymaker and Francis Schiller, *The Founders of Neurology* (Springfield, Ill., 1970), p. 33.

6. From Bernard Hollander, *In Search of the Soul* (London, 1920), pp. 288–9.

7. Gall, cited in ibid., pp. 240, 238, 241.

8. The most important recent defender of Wernicke's views is Norman Geschwind. See "Carl Wernicke, The Breslau School and the History of Aphasia," in his *Selected Papers on Language and the Brain* (Boston, 1974), pp. 42–72. See also his famous paper on the disconnection syndrome in the same volume, pp. 105–236, and my discussion of that and related work in *The Invention of Memory* (New York, 1989), pp. 30–56. See, too, Anne Harrington, "Beyond Phre-

nology: Localization Theory in the Modern Era," in *The Enchanted Loom*, pp. 207–15.

9. K. Goldstein, *Aftereffects of Brain Injuries in War: Their Evaluation and Treatment* (New York, 1942), p. 71. For a well-known but rather misleading critique of Goldstein, see Norman Geschwind, "The Paradoxical Position of Kurt Goldstein in the History of Aphasia," in *Selected Papers*, pp. 62–72. Geschwind does not discuss Goldstein's philosophical and psychological views, which I explore in the following chapters.

10. See Lina Bolzoni, "The Play of Images: The Art of Memory from Its Origins to the Seventeenth Century," in *The Enchanted Loom*, pp. 16–26.

11. Alexandr Luria, *The Mind of a Mnemonist* (London, 1975), pp. 30, 35.

12. Gilles de la Tourette, "Étude sur une affection nerveuse caractérisée par de l'incoordination motrice accompagnée d'écholalie et de coprolalie," *Archive Neurologique* 9 (1885): 174–6.

13. Ibid., p. 42.

14. Ibid., pp. 179–80.

15. Luria, *Mnemonist*, p. 115.

16. Ibid., p. 114.

17. Cited in Oliver Sacks, *The Man Who Mistook His Wife for a Hat* (New York, 1985), p. 96.

II   The Counterfeit Leg

1. Cited in Bernard Hollander, *In Search of the Soul* (London, 1920), pp. 158–9.

2. All subsequent quotations about this case from G. Deny and P. Camus, "Sur une forme d'hypocondrie aberrante due à la perte de la conscience du corps," *Revue Neurologique* 9 (15 May 1905): 32ff.

3. Pierre Bonnier, *Vertiges* (Paris, 1893). See, too, Bonnier's "L'aschématie," *Revue Neurologique* 1905: 54ff.

4. Henry Head, *Studies in Neurology*, vol. II (London, 1920), p. 605.

5. Ibid., pp. 605–6.

6. Ibid., p. 754.

7. Paul Schilder, *The Image and Appearance of the Human Body* (London, 1935), p. 287.

8. M. J. Babinski, "Contribution à l'étude des troubles mentaux dans

✓

l'hemiplégie organique cérébrale (anosognosie)," *Société de Neurologie*, 11 June 1914: 112–15.

9. Oliver Sacks, *A Leg to Stand On* (New York, 1984), pp. 125, 67, 85–6.

10. Cited by Babinski himself in "Contribution": 114–15.

11. T. Shallice, *From Neuropsychology to Mental Structure* (Cambridge, Eng., 1988), p. 327.

12. Sacks, *A Leg*, pp. 152–3.

13. See J. Lapresle and J. M. Verret, "Syndrome d'Anton-Babinsky avec reconnaissance du membre supérieur gauche lors de sa vision dans le miroir," *Revue Neurologique* 134 (11) 1978: 709–13.

14. See R. Garcin and Hadji-Dino Varay, "Documents pour servir à l'étude des troubles du schéma corporel," *Revue Neurologique* 69 (1938): 498–510.

15. P. J. Kellman and E. S. Spelke, "Perception of Partly Occluded Objects in Infancy," *Cognitive Psychology* 15 (1983): 521.

16. Shallice, *Neuropsychology*, p. 400.

17. See E. Bisiach and C. Luzzatti, "Unilateral Neglect of Representational Space," *Cortex* 14 (1978): 129–33.

18. J. M. Hull, *Touching the Rock: An Experience of Blindness* (London, 1990), p. 48.

19. Ibid., p. 52.

20. Ibid., p. 104.

III In a World Without Time

1. Korsakov's original papers were published in 1887 and 1890. *Arkh. Psikiat. Nevrol.* 1887, vol. 9, no. 2: 16–38; no. 3: 1–14. *Arch. psychiat.* (Berlin) 21 (1890): 669–704. Parts of the papers are translated in Gantt and Muncie, *Bull. Johns Hopkins Hospital* 70 (1942): 467–87.

2. Oliver Sacks, *The Man Who Mistook His Wife for a Hat* (New York, 1985), p. 28.

3. W. B. Scoville and Brenda Milner, "Loss of Recent Memory After Bilateral Hippocampal Lesions," *Journal of Neurology, Neurosurgery and Psychiatry* 20 (1957): 11–21.

4. See E. Tulving, "Episodic and Semantic Memory," in *Organization of Memory*, ed. E. Tulving and W. Donaldson (New York, 1972). Also see T. Shallice, *From Neuropsychology to Mental Structure* (Cambridge, Eng., 1988).

5. All subsequent quotations about this case from H. Mabille and A.

Pitres, "Sur un cas d'amnésie de fixation post-apoplectique ayant persisté pendant vingt-trois ans," *Revue de Médecine* (April 1913): 119–31.

6. J. M. Hull, *Touching the Rock: An Experience of Blindness* (London, 1990), pp. 71–2, 61.

7. K. Goldstein, "L'analyse de l'aphasie et l'étude de l'essence du langage," *Journal de Psychologie: Normale et Pathologique* XXX (1933): 482.

8. Ibid., 483.

9. A. Gelb, "Remarques générales sur l'utilisation des données pathologiques pour la psychologie et la philosophie du langage," *Journal de Psychologie: Normale et Pathologique* XXX (1933): 415, 418.

10. See G. M. Edelman, "Group Selection and Phasic Reentrant Signaling: A Theory of Higher Brain Function," in *The Mindful Brain*, ed. G. M. Edelman and V. B. Mountcastle (Cambridge, Mass., 1978), pp. 51–100.

11. W. J. Clancey, review of Rosenfield's *The Invention of Memory*, in *The Journal of Artificial Intelligence* 50 (1991):241–84.

12. See P. Eckhorn, R. Bauer, W. Jordan, M. Brusch, W. Kruse, M. Munk, and H. J. Reitboeck, "Coherent Oscillations: A Mechanism of Feature Linking in the Visual Cortex?" *Biological Cybernetics* 60 (1988): 121–30. The conclusion is from C. M. Gray and W. Singer, "Stimulus-Specific Neuronal Oscillations in Orientation Columns of Cat Visual Cortex," *PNAS* 86 (1989): 1698–1702.

13. J. W. Papez, "A Proposed Mechanism of Emotion," *Archives of Neurology and Psychiatry* XXXIII (1937): 725–43.

14. Heinrich Klüver and Paul Bucy, *Trans. Amer. Neur. Ass.* 65 (1939): 170–5. When they delivered their paper to the American Neurological Association in 1939, they made no mention of Papez's earlier, and considerably more important, paper. Papez took part in the discussion and did not mention his paper either.

15. Israel Rosenfield, *The Invention of Memory* (New York, 1988), pp. 167–70, 222–3, n. 11.

IV Language

1. From Frederic Bateman, *On Aphasia or Loss of Speech and the Localisation of the Faculty of Articulate Language* (London, 1890); diagram on p. 38, text pp. 40–1.

2. J. M. Charcot, "Leçons sur les maladies du système nerveux," in

Oeuvres Complètes, vol. III, ed. Babinski, Bernard, Féré, Guinon, Marie et Gilles de la Tourette (Paris, 1890), pp. 189–90.

3. Monsieur A's case is discussed in ibid., pp. 179–88.
4. Henry Head, *Aphasia and Kindred Disorders*, vol. I (London, 1926), p. 525.
5. Ibid., pp. 521–2.
6. J. M. Hull, *Touching the Rock: An Experience of Blindness* (London, 1990), p. 73.
7. See A. Gelb and K. Goldstein, "Über Farbennamenamnesie, usw," *Psychologische Forschung* VI (1925): 127–86. The quotation in the text is from A. Gelb, "Remarques générales sur l'utilisation des données pathologiques pour la psychologie et la philosophie du langage," *Journal de Psychologie: Normale et Pathologique* XXX (1933): 410.
8. Ibid., 412–13.
9. Ibid., 416.
10. K. Goldstein, *Language and Language Disturbances* (New York, 1948), p. 61.
11. Ibid., p. 62.
12. K. Goldstein, "L'analyse de l'aphasie et l'étude de l'essence du langage," *Journal de Psychologie: Normale et Pathologique* XXX (1933): 484, 481.
13. Head, *Aphasia*, vol. I, pp. 119–20.
14. Jacques Mehler and Emmanuel Dupoux, *Naître Humain* (Paris, 1990), p. 87.
15. Ibid.
16. Ibid., p. 81.
17. See my *The Invention of Memory*, pp. 30–57, for an extensive discussion of "disconnection syndromes."
18. Melissa Bowerman, "Inducing the Latent Structure of Language," in *The Development of Language and Language Researchers: Essays in Honor of Roger Brown*, ed. Frank S. Kessel (Hillsdale, N.J., 1988), pp. 27–8.
19. The classic study of language acquisition is Roger Brown, *A First Language* (Cambridge, Mass., 1973). See, too, Peter A. and Jill G. Villiers, *Early Language* (Cambridge, Mass., 1979), esp. chap. 3, 4, and 5.
20. See Paul Fletcher, *A Child's Learning of English* (Oxford, 1985), p. 116.
21. See Anne Dunlea, *Vision and the Emergence of Meaning: Blind and*

Sighted Children's Early Language (Cambridge, Eng., 1989). Note esp. p. 103: "[C]onsider the event encoded by the adult sentence 'George rolls the ball to Mary.' A sighted child at the two-word stage commenting on this is likely to encode 'ball,' 'ball roll' or even 'George roll ball' (assuming that perception of an object undergoing a change of state is the likely element to be encoded . . .). Now consider this from the blind child's perspective. If Mary is blind, she has immediate knowledge of her own existence and she can discover, after the ball has made contact with her, that the object in question is a ball. Note that she must explore her environment *after the event* has been completed in order to identify the ball. If a sighted child encodes 'ball' in this situation, she seems to be encoding an object in change (or at least that is one possible interpretation). We can't say the same is true for the blind child—it seems to be that 'ball' is an identification of an object just encountered. The concept 'roll to' is virtually meaningless for a blind child."

22. See ibid., pp. 106–9. Note, for example: "the sudden burst in vocabulary growth, which seems to correlate with a change in *use* of words for sighted children, was either not present for the blind subjects, or, . . . was simply a rapid increase in the number of terms with little change in their use." Note, too, the following comments, p. 162: "[F]rom a cognitive perspective, the constrained pattern of conceptual development supports an epistemological theory that is both biogenetic and interactionist. The child's own actions on the world, and especially his observation of it, are essential to the construction of a meaningful concept of that world. From a linguistic perspective, the blind children's development indicates that what appears to be a universal ontogenetic progression in the acquisition of language cannot be fully actualized in the absence of a supporting conceptual framework. If anything, the importance of visual information in the emergence of meaning has been considerably underestimated, for it functions as a vital stimulus for activating the processes which underlie linguistic development, at least in the early stages."

23. Susan Goldin-Meadow and Heidi Feldman, "The Development of Language-like Communication Without Language Model," *Science* 22 (July 1977): 401–3.

24. D. Bickerton, "Creole Languages," *Scientific American*, July 1983, p. 119. See, too, Bickerton's most recent work on this subject—a

defense of the idea of an innate universal grammar—*Language and Species* (Chicago, 1990).

25. See Bruner and Feldman's review of Bickerton's *The Roots of Language* in *The New York Review of Books*, June 24, 1982, pp. 34–6, and the exchange of letters between Bickerton and Bruner and Feldman in the issue of September 23, 1982, p. 62. Note, in particular, the following remarks by Bruner and Feldman: "There remains, however, the very general question raised by Bickerton's work. There appear to be four distinctions that recur in simple syntactic form in virtually all Creoles, and they appear in the 'errors' of children's speech where simple forms are not available in their cultural language—Specific-Nonspecific, State-Process, Punctual-Nonpunctual, and Causative-Noncausative. Where they are available, they tend to be acquired errorlessly. Diffusion could not possibly account for their presence in children's language. We doubted in our review whether a 'bioprogram' alone produced them in various Creoles. Our opinion was that they could more readily arise in response to universal cultural requirements. And if they could come about by diffusion, indeed, why just this set of distinctions?"

26. Wilhelm von Humboldt, *On Language: The Diversity of Human Language-Structure and Its Influence on the Mental Development of Mankind*, trans. Peter Heath, with an introduction by Hans Aarsleff (Cambridge, Eng., 1988), pp. 51–2.

27. Noam Chomsky, *Language and Mind* (New York, 1968), p. 24. See, too, Chomsky's *Current Issues in Linguistic Theory*, pp. 19ff: "A generative grammar . . . is an attempt to represent, in a precise manner, certain aspects of the *form* of language, and a particular theory of generative grammar is an attempt to specify those aspects of form that are a common human possession—in Humboldtian terms, one might identify this with the underlying general form of all language."

28. Dan I. Slobin quotes this phrase from notes he took during a lecture by Chomsky, in "From the Garden of Eden to the Tower of Babel," in *The Development of Language*, p. 12.

29. Noam Chomsky, *Rules and Representations* (New York, 1980), p. 53.

30. Ibid., p. 215.

31. Humboldt, *On Language*, p. 58.

32. Ibid., p. 59.

33. R. C. Collingwood, *The Principles of Art* (New York, 1958), p. 257. I owe this passage to William J. Clancey, who used it in his review of my *The Invention of Memory*, in *The Journal of Artificial Intelligence*.

V Multiple Personalities

1. William James, *The Principles of Psychology* (reprint, Cambridge, Mass., 1981), pp. 1, 358.
2. See E. Tranel and A. R. Damasio, "Knowledge Without Awareness: An Autonomic Index of Facial Recognition by Prosopagnostics," *Science* 228: 1453–4. An earlier study was reported by R. M. Bauer in *Neuropsychologia* 22: 457–69.
3. James, *Principles*, pp. 359–62. The case was originally reported by William S. Plumer in *Harper's Magazine*, May 1860, and more extensively by Weir Mitchell in *Transactions of the College of Physicians of Philadelphia*, April 4, 1888. I have here used James's version throughout.
4. Morton Prince, *The Dissociation of a Personality: A Biographical Study in Abnormal Psychology* (reprint, New York, 1969), p. 14.
5. Morton Prince, *Clinical and Experimental Studies in Personality* (New York, 1970), p. 235.
6. Ibid., p. 190.
7. Ibid., pp. 147–50.
8. Ibid., pp. 153–4.
9. Sigmund Freud, "The Unconscious," in *The Standard Edition of the Complete Psychological Works of Sigmund Freud*, vol. XIV, p. 187.
10. J. M. Hull, *Touching the Rock: An Experience of Blindness* (London, 1990), p. 14.
11. Ibid., pp. 19, 103, 145.
12. Ibid., p. 119.
13. Ibid., p. 38.
14. K. Goldstein, "L'analyse de l'aphasie et l'étude de l'essence du langage," *Journal de Psychologie: Normale et Pathologique* XXX (1933): 489.
15. Henry Head, *Aphasia and Kindred Disorders*, vol. I (London, 1926), p. 544.

Index

Index

Head, Henry, 46–8, 84–5, 94–6, 101–2, 107, 140
hippocampus, 71–3, 85
Histoire naturelle de l'âme (La Mettrie), 36
history, 86–7
holism, 24
Homme machine, L' (La Mettrie), 36
Hubel, David, 24
Hull, John, 64, 77, 96, 133, 136–8
Humbolt, Wilhelm von, 114–17
hypothalamus, 86

infancy, 60–2; categorization in, 102–4
inhibition, 134

James, William, 122, 124

Kellman, P. J., 61–2
Kleist, Heinrich von, 79
Klüver, Heinrich, 86
knowledge, 5, 7, 13; acquisition of, 61–2; fixed categories of, 81, 82; frame of reference for, 46; language and, 56; memory and, 9, 21, 22, 28, 69; naming and, 98; senses

and, 37; stored, 38; subjectivity of, 27, 48, 85; time sense and, 81; without awareness, 123n
Korsakov, Sergei, 67, 68
Korsakov's syndrome, 68–9, 71, 73, 80

La Mettrie, Julien Offroy de, 36–7
language, 34, 87–119, 129; acquisition of, 62, 102–9; concrete use of, 96–7, 99, 100; consciousness and, 53, 87, 96, 107–9; gestural, 108–13; innate rules theory of, 113–19; knowledge and, 56, 104–5; and loss of body image, 43; memory images and, 37–8; nature and basis of, 35; and self-centered world view, 78; and subjectivity, 112–13; symbolic, 107–11, 121
Leonardo da Vinci, 13
light, nature of, 13
limbic system, 45n, 85–6
localizations, 15–20, 25
Locke, John, 9, 37
Loewi, Otto, 23
logic, combinatory, 29
long-term memory, 69, 73, 80; conversion from short-term memory to, 71; habitual responses versus, 75–6; loss of, 78–9; in multiple